# SOUTH HILL
## WASHINGTON

· A COMMUNITY HISTORY ·

Carl Vest and Members of the South Hill Historical Society
*Edited by Hans Zeiger and Jerry Bates*

Published by The History Press
Charleston, SC
www.historypress.com

Copyright © 2021 by the South Hill Historical Society
All rights reserved

First published 2021

Manufactured in the United States

ISBN 9781467145039

Library of Congress Control Number: 2020948447

*Notice*: The information in this book is true and complete to the best of our knowledge. It is offered without guarantee on the part of the author or The History Press. The author and The History Press disclaim all liability in connection with the use of this book.

All rights reserved. No part of this book may be reproduced or transmitted in any form whatsoever without prior written permission from the publisher except in the case of brief quotations embodied in critical articles and reviews.

# CONTENTS

Foreword, by Hans Zeiger     5

1. Coming to the Hill     11
2. Farmers     25
3. Neighborhoods     41
4. Schools     55
5. Meridian Avenue and Other Roads     70
6. Rural Life     87
7. The Grange, the Old Mill and the Drag Strip:
      Cultural Roots on the Hill     109
8. Development     130
9. Public Places and Services     149
10. South Hill in the Twenty-First Century     172

South Hill History: A Timeline     183
Acknowledgements     187
Bibliography     189
Index     199
About the South Hill Historical Society     205
About the Author and Editors     207

# FOREWORD

This is the first published history of South Hill, Washington, but the effort that has gone into this project has spanned at least two decades. This book is only possible because a small group of South Hill citizens decided, in 2001, to found the South Hill Historical Society. It is good that they did so at that time. Not only did they recruit friends to join the society and take part in its gatherings, but they proceeded to assemble a truly impressive body of oral history. One only needs to turn to the bibliography at the end of this book to see how far they went to record the memories of men and women who remember the Hill when it was rural. "Early on," wrote Carl Vest, "we decided to video tape interviews with older people on the Hill. Paul Hackett took the lead in this, as he had more contacts than either Ben Peters or me. I remember helping him with some interviews with people like Ward Bradley and John Thun (both now gone). He used a VHS system. After most of the interviews, Paul made me a copy. I collected these and used them for writing." Carl launched a long-running series of articles in the *Puyallup Herald*, while Jerry Bates saw to it that the pages of the South Hill Historical Society newsletter were filled with additional material of historical interest—firsthand recollections, letters, reports on the proceedings of Historical Society meetings and much more.

To thousands who have known South Hill as home, the place is rich with stories. This is true for today's residents, whether they live in neighborhoods filled with single-family homes and apartments; commute to and from

# Foreword

work via Shaw Road, Meridian Avenue or Canyon Road; or have a high school mascot that is a ram or a jaguar. It was certainly true for the men and women who experienced South Hill in its earlier days. The South Hill tradition runs deep.

My own family has a stake in South Hill that dates back nearly seventy years. My grandparents Ed and Wilma Zeiger bought five acres in 1952 in what used to be called the Rabbit Farms, near 122$^{nd}$ Street. They raised their kids there in the woods and watched the hill grow up around them. Their property is on a hill of its own, and Grandma Wilma wanted a house on top of the hill with a view of the mountain. So, they built a new house in 1999, and the view was wonderful. Grandma Wilma passed away in 2004, but my grandpa Ed still lives up there at the age of ninety-one.

South Hill is not an official city, despite efforts to incorporate more than two decades ago. South Hill is actually a cluster of residential areas, some of which are in the City of Puyallup and some of which are in unincorporated Pierce County. As you will see in this book, there's really nothing new about South Hill residents' propensity to associate in neighborhoods. Originally, the Hill was divided into several distinct neighborhoods, whose names still mostly exist in recognizable landmarks. South Hill people got to know each other in their respective neighborhoods. Three of the neighborhoods formed around small independent schools that each had their own school boards: Firgrove, Woodland and Puyallup Heights. The Puyallup Heights neighborhood encompassed today's mall area. From there, Firgrove was to the south, Woodland was to the west and Rabbit Farms was to the east. Locations on the Hill acquired familiar names, such as Willows Corner, where 39$^{th}$ Street meets Meridian Avenue today; it is marked by landmarks like the Willows Dance Hall, Willows Tavern and Willows Lumber.

Early South Hill settlers were generally farmers, and many of them were from German American families with names like Kupfer, Mosolf, Barth, Patzner, Glaser and Muehler. Many Hill residents in the first half of the twentieth century worked in the Valley, while others commuted to Tacoma. My grandparents bought their place from an English immigrant named Robert Newcomb who jumped ship from a British vessel in Canada, moved to the Hill in 1930 and built a little house on his property. He raised chickens, but he made most of his modest living by working seasonal shifts at Hunt's Cannery in downtown Puyallup.

South Hill was rural and simple, and the people were sometimes poor. The community's wealth was found in the friendships that flourished here.

# Foreword

A wave of families moved to the Hill in the 1950s and 1960s, during the postwar boom. The people who came during these years set down roots on the Hill. Many of them started businesses here. My grandparents came here during that time. The Boy Scout troop that my dad and his brothers joined—and that my grandfather helped lead—was founded by George Newcomer in 1951 at Woodland School. It helped accommodate some of the new families who were moving into the area.

As growth continued, John R. Rogers High School opened in 1968, forever altering the relationship between the Hill and the Valley and laying down a new anchor for South Hill pride and identity.

As more people called South Hill home in the 1970s, there was little official coordination. There were tensions between community leaders and the county over development. A housing boom commenced, and the Meridian Corridor became more crowded.

Growth happened quickly. By the late 1980s, South Hill became the focus of shopping in the greater Puyallup area. When the mall opened in 1988, much of the shopping shifted from places like Hi Ho Shopping Center and various smaller stores in the Valley to larger stores on the Hill, which continued to expand along Meridian Avenue over time.

South Hill has also had a few major community gathering spots that opened in recent decades. The first was Pierce College Puyallup, which was founded in 1989. The second was the Mel Korum Family YMCA, which opened in 2000 and has really become a central place for activity. The third was the second high school on the Hill, Emerald Ridge, on the edge of the Sunrise development, which also opened in 2000.

It is interesting to consider that South Hill lagged behind the Puyallup Valley in terms of its major development by basically one hundred years. Ezra Meeker platted downtown Puyallup in 1877; most of what we know as South Hill today was developed after 1977.

For generations, South Hill has attracted people with its relatively affordable housing and its good schools, among other things. Today, young working families move here, contributing to the Puget Sound economy; they are blue-collar workers, service workers, tech workers and military personnel from Joint Base Lewis-McChord. Along with the growth of South Hill as a bedroom community, there has been continued growth in local businesses and schools. There are now sixteen elementary schools, junior highs and high schools on the Hill. With growth there have also been a number of social challenges for the South Hill community, including traffic congestion and crime.

FOREWORD

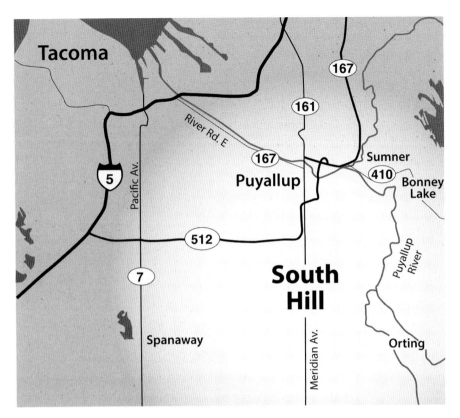

South Hill, a growing community in Pierce County, Washington. *Courtesy of Jerry Bates and the South Hill Historical Society.*

As South Hill continues to develop, its residents can each do their part to preserve its roots and cultivate a sense of place in the rising generation. We each must do everything we can to make this—our home—better. I would suggest three specific things that can be done to make South Hill better.

The first has to do with teaching newer South Hill residents the history of this community. As things change, it is important to cultivate an awareness of how things were in the past so that we can have a sense of continuity. The South Hill Historical Society has been a labor of love for a dedicated group of men and women, and the best thing we can do to reward their commitment is continue it into a new generation.

The second thing that we need to do is preserve some of the older landmarks here. You have seen some of the old street names on street signs, like Glaser Road, Patzner Road, Ball-Wood Road and Muehler-Berger Road. There are old houses and old landmarks that exist if you look for

## Foreword

them, and this book will serve as a guide to many of them. One worthwhile thing that we could do is preserve the old Firgrove School, which was built in 1935. It would be wonderful if community groups could purchase the red-brick building for use rather than allowing it to be demolished. People need physical reminders of their history.

Finally, we need to initiate a new era of civic engagement on South Hill. We need visionaries with imagination and enthusiasm who can rally their neighbors to try new things. As more and more housing crowds the Hill, we need leaders who will protect and cultivate outlets for public gathering, recreation and celebration. We need new ways for young professionals on the Hill to meet one another and get involved in worthy causes that shape the future of the community. As baby boomers retire, we need new outlets for volunteerism. And as established institutions look for ways to attract a new generation of members or customers, we need a renewal of pride in this special Pacific Northwest place.

Whether South Hill will ever be a city of its own remains a topic for discussion. City or not, it is home to thousands who have chosen to live here because they love it. As you will see in the pages that follow, Carl Vest and the men and women of the South Hill Historical Society have a deep love for this place, and we hope that this book will help you deepen your own.

Hans Zeiger
South Hill, Washington
December 8, 2020

# 1
# COMING TO THE HILL

South Hill was once part of a major trail system that connected the eastern and western tribes of the Pacific Northwest. It was used for purposes of trade and to communicate, hunt for game, and gather resources. Historians usually refer to it as the Ancient Klickitat Trail. A significant trail ran east to west along the path of today's Military Road, not far from the busy corridor of Highway 512.

South Hill was regarded by the Puyallup people as a place to find cedar, gather roots and berries, hunt and train young men. People fished on Clover Creek and pursued elk through present-day Graham and Elk Plain.

According to the Puyallup Tribe, South Hill was the tribe's "abundant resource" for many things, including berries, black bear, elk, deer and roots. The young males were trained all over South Hill, including today's Bradley Lake area. According to Brandon Reynon of the Puyallup Tribe, the Hill had no documented permanent villages; rather, it had hunting camps equipped with traveling shelters constructed of split cedar planks or tule mats and strapping that could be torn down and reassembled. The most important resource the Hill offered was probably the cedar tree. Nicole Barandon, also of the tribe, related how absolutely essential cedar bark was for them. It provided clothing, baskets, hats and numerous utensils; it was even woven into mountain goat wool blankets. The cedar bark was also used as bug repellant—"mosquitos and bugs hated it," she said. The trees were carefully stripped of small areas of bark so as not to kill them, and elder trees were spared. The tribe's dugout canoes were made of fallen cedar logs. Barandon said the trees with rotted centers saved the labor of hollowing big logs. These techniques for canoe building and stripping bark are still used by the tribe today, according to Barandon and Reynon.

Areas to the south of South Hill were believed to be the native home of the *tsiakos*, according to Reynon. The tsiakos was a bigfoot-like being with red eyes that was said to steal children. The story of the tsiakos was told in the region throughout the generations in part, it is said, to keep children inside at night.

Native Americans were still active on the Hill when the period of pioneer settlement began. Records from settler groups like the Hudson Bay Company document the presence of a Native population around the 1840s, but these Native organizations were apparently small and generally did not remain after the influx of settlers. The old growth trees that the Puyallup people had modified as trail markers were eventually cut down by timber companies. Three old growth trees remain near the Orting Soldiers Home.

One remnant of the Ancient Klickitat Trail remains, though its name, Military Road, dates back to the Treaty Wars of 1855 and 1856. These wars were brought on by tensions surrounding treaty negotiations between the federal government and the Northwest tribes. During the war, the trail become a supply route linking Fort Maloney on the Puyallup River with Fort Steilacoom. Tribal warriors raided supply parties, and there were multiple skirmishes along the route.

## New Settlement

During the 1840s and 1850s, recognized settlements started to appear in the south Puget Sound area. The Donation Land Claim Act drew people to the Washington Territory, but there is no record that any claim was ever filed on South Hill. There are recorded claims along the Puyallup River, in the Spanaway region, and at other points near South Hill, but none on the highland itself.

Immigrants headed to the Pacific Northwest in ever increasing numbers throughout the 1850s. In the early days, settlers entered the Puget Sound region either by water or overland from the Fort Vancouver area. If they came by water, Steilacoom was the common port of entry. If they came over land, depending on the period, the path was also from Fort Vancouver but was by the Columbia-Cowlitz River system and with wagons or pack animals. Either way, emigrants ended up in the Steilacoom area with easy access to points inland.

An exception was the Naches Pass Trail settlers, who came in 1853.

## Longmire-Biles

On October 8, 1853, a small wagon train crossed South Hill, bringing settlers to the Puget Sound region. That event is noteworthy, as it was the first emigrant wagon train to move through the Naches Pass of the Cascade Mountains, traveling on what is now called the North Fork of the Oregon Trail.

The Naches Pass Trail has existed for centuries. It originated in Walla Walla, traversed the Cascades through Naches Pass, descended the western slopes of the mountains near Bonney Lake, crossed the Puyallup River and then passed over South Hill from the Northeast to the Southwest. The trail then went through Parkland and ended in Steilacoom.

The wagon train that crossed South Hill is generally labeled the Longmire-Biles party. It was formed near Umatilla, Oregon, when two separate groups arrived from the east, both moving along the Oregon Trail, and decided to combine and complete their journey together. Both were headed for Fort Steilacoom in the Puget Sound area. One had been captained by James Longmire and the other by James Biles. The number of vehicles participating in the journey still remains in dispute, but a collection of about thirty-five wagons appears to be a reasonable estimate. Also, the number of people in the party is not accurately known, but historians estimate they numbered around 170.

The James Longmire party left Cedar Rapids, Iowa, in May 1853. Some five months and two thousand miles later, on September 8, they crossed the Columbia River near Umatilla, Oregon. It took another three weeks for them to cross the area we know today as central Washington. They reached Summit Prairie, now named Government Meadows, around October 1. That location put the pioneers at the summit of the Cascade Mountains in Naches Pass.

The train then went down the west side of the Cascades, across the Puyallup River and over South Hill in a week. The settlers climbed onto South Hill after crossing the Puyallup River through the ford at Van Ogle's homestead. Not much of the path up the Hill still exists, but their point of arrival at the top is identified by a marker near Ridgecrest Elementary School on Military Road. From that point, the direction of the old trail was generally west, toward present-day Rogers High School. In fact, the school

The Naches Pass fork of the Oregon Trail was followed by the 1853 Longmire-Biles wagon train, the first American settlers to Puget Sound to cross over the Cascades. *Courtesy of Jerry Bates and the South Hill Historical Society.*

was built directly on the path. There are markers at Rogers and on both sides of the campus that show where the road existed. From the school site, the path generally moved in a southwesterly direction. It left the Hill near Woodland Avenue and 160th Street.

The party reached the Mahon Ranch on Clover Creek on October 8. Today, that location is the site of the Brookdale Golf Course. At that point, they made contact with Fort Steilacoom. After a period of rest, the group disbanded as an organized entity.

The South Hill part of the Naches Trail has mostly been covered over by development, but its various locations can be generally identified by a number of road signs throughout the area labeled "Military Road." Moreover, its location is illustrated on numerous old maps and in written materials held by various archives.

Over several years, Pierce County took steps to recognize and mark portions of the old trail where it crossed South Hill. On October 11, 2001, the county dedicated the South Hill Heritage Corridor and installed a number of historic markers throughout the community to show where the trail existed at various points. Also, the South Hill Community Plan, dated December 11, 2002, recognized the importance of the Heritage Corridor. The document states that, as a matter of county policy, it will "actively pursue the opportunity to link the South Hill Heritage Corridor with the Naches Trail from Walla Walla to Steilacoom."

Then, in 2009, President Obama signed into law the Omnibus Public Land Management Act of 2009, requiring that the secretary of the interior undertake a study of the western routes used by emigrants to determine the feasibility and suitability of designating one or more as components of existing national historic trails. Specifically listed in the law was the Naches Pass Trail, which could become a part of the current Oregon National Historic Trail. As of this writing, the National Park Service's feasibility study for adding the Naches Pass Trail to the Oregon National Historic Trail remains in progress.

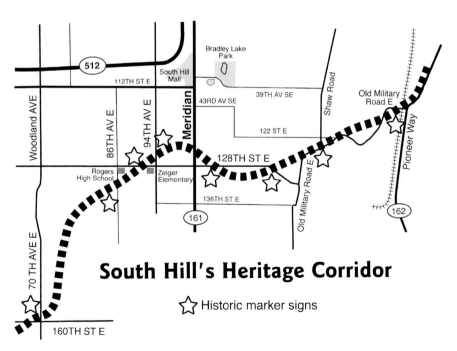

The route followed by the Longmire-Biles wagon train over South Hill, the North Fork of the Oregon Trail. *Courtesy of Jerry Bates and the South Hill Historical Society.*

South Hill, Washington

## The Ballard Survey

South Hill was first surveyed in 1872 by William Rankin Ballard. Ballard was born in Ohio in 1847. His father brought him to Oregon in 1858. Subsequently, he studied at several schools, achieving proficiency in civil engineering. He taught school for a while but eventually was appointed a contract as a federal deputy land surveyor.

The mapping of the Pacific Northwest began in 1851 with the establishment of a control point near the confluence of the Columbia and Willamette Rivers just outside of Portland, Oregon. From that point, townships were established on a north–south meridian line and an east–west range line. That process was in keeping with the system specified by Congress in 1785 called the Rectangular Survey System or the Public Land Survey System. Tracts of land were divided into geometric shapes that were approximately six miles across on each side starting at the control point. Each thirty-six-square-mile unit was called a township. South Hill is located four townships to the east of the control point and nineteen townships north; it is usually designated by the shorthand notation T19R4E.

The Federal General Land Office (GLO) controlled the distribution of federal land in the 1800s. GLO was responsible for mapping the land areas to be distributed so that proper title could be established and maintained. In 1872, it issued to William Ballard Contract No. 138 to survey two townships, T19R3E and T19R4E. This thirty-six-square-mile plot comprised South Hill and the township directly to the west.

It can be said that Ballard "chained" South Hill. He used a so-called Gunter's chain to measure distances. A Gunter chain was a sixty-six-foot-long set of links that was dragged along each township line to establish boundaries. These routes were determined mathematically and did not necessarily follow natural contours and existing trails. As for specific locations and directions, a solar compass was used, as the magnetic compass was not considered reliable. A typical survey party consisted of six people: the surveyor, two chainmen, a person to read the compass, a person to mark the corners and a cook.

Plats from the Ballard survey show only three established home sites in Township 19, the area we now call South Hill. All three were located near the pathway of the Naches Pass Trail. William Weiderhold was noted as living in Section 8. In today's terms, his location was around 112th Street and 74th Avenue. Charles Miller was recorded as living right beside the old trail on a line between Sections 16 and 17. Today, we would describe that

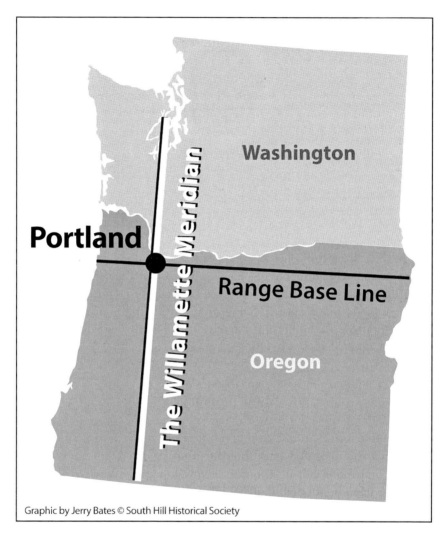

The Willamette Meridian and Range Base Line, the basis for Pacific Northwest Surveying. *Courtesy of Jerry Bates and the South Hill Historical Society.*

position as being around 125th Street and 86th Avenue. Anton Dumblar was just south of Miller, at what today is near 136th Street and 86th Avenue.

So, other than Native Americans, these three individuals appear to have been the first people to inhabit South Hill. Since these names do not appear in future records about the Hill, it could have been that these early people were squatters and had no legal claim to their locations. Perhaps they were forced out as others came into the area. This remains a mystery.

As for Ballard, he left contract surveying in 1876 and went into maritime work. It was in 1883 that he turned to speculating in real estate. He bought seven hundred acres of land on Salmon Bay in Seattle and started subdividing it into building lots. He sold these lots from time to time to further other business interests. This location is known to this day as the Ballard neighborhood.

## Settling and Surveying

Land ownership records provide the names and locations of many early pioneers on South Hill. Records started being kept in the 1840s, when the Northwest became a part of the United States and when boundary lines were established in a treaty with Great Britain. Land titles then flowed from the federal government to individuals in basically three ways. One of the earliest of these land titles was the Donation Land Claim Act of 1850 (DLC). Basically, it was a law that protected settlers who had come into the Oregon Territory before the boundary disputes were settled. A second statute was the Homestead Act of 1862, which was used by many settlers on South Hill. Third, some pioneers simply purchased land from the federal government.

Settlers started to move to South Hill shortly after the Ballard survey. Technically, there were no DLCs on South Hill, but within Township 19, where South Hill is located, three DLC claims were made. In 1875, Thomas Headly patented 320 acres apportioned between Sections 24 and 25, and in 1876, Daniel Lane claimed 367 acres that were distributed between Sections 13, 19, 24 and 25. Both the Headly and Lane holdings were located along the Puyallup River and in the valley east of South Hill. Lastly, in 1878, George Brown obtained 160 acres spread between Sections 6 and 31. These areas were located just to the west of South Hill, Section 6 being in the present-day area of Summit and Section 31 being near Frederickson. These dates are when the titles were transferred, which verified that the pioneers had moved onto the land several years before.

The Homestead Act of 1862 was used by many early pioneers. Homestead records show that it was during the 1870s that settlers began to move onto the eastern slopes of South Hill. The driving force for this move was probably that all the good land in the river valley had been taken. Carl Muehler, one of the first to settle on the Hill, used the Homestead Act in 1879 to acquire eighty acres in Section 22. Using today's point of reference, this plot was located near the intersection of 152nd Street and 110th Avenue. In 1879, Joseph Geiger, using the same law, acquired eighty acres in Section 14, an area around the present-day Tacoma Water Reservoir. Fritz Balck also acquired eighty acres in Section 12, an area on the hill above McMillin, in 1879.

The third way some settlers obtained land was through outright purchase. In the 1870s, several South Hill pioneers did just that. The first purchase was recorded in 1876, when Edward Sane bought 160 acres in Section 13, just east of today's McMillan water reservoir near 122nd Avenue East and 152nd Street East. In 1877, both James Hall and James Leonard bought 160 acres in Section 14, also near the reservoir. In 1877, Daniel Woolery purchased 160 acres in Section 24.

The early pioneers tended to put down roots on the northern part of the plateau. While there were some farms established toward the south, they were not as numerous as those just outside of Puyallup.

There are accounts from early settlers that declare that they did not even know Puyallup existed when they first arrived. Records describe Native Americans taking some settlers to the ridge lines and pointing out the existence of Puyallup.

In general, early settlers accessed the east side of the Hill from the Puyallup River and the west side by the Naches Pass Trail, later known as the Military Road. Movements during the 1850s, 1860s and certainly into the 1870s tended to fit this pattern. Stories of events during the Indian Wars, for example, focus on engagements along the Military Road.

In 1889, a five-mile stretch of what is now Meridian Avenue was surveyed, and the field notes written by that survey team give some clues as to what the Hill was like. The work started around the present-day intersection of Meridian and Pioneer Avenues, then the Puyallup city line, and proceeded south. The first quarter mile was cut through cleared land, ending around today's fairgrounds. The next quarter mile was also clear, but it was noted that a forest was on one side of the track. Total woodland was encountered beyond the half-mile point, and to continue, it was necessary to clear a work path. At the one-mile point, an identification marker was created by notching two trees, a forty-inch-diameter fir and a twelve-inch cottonwood.

After the first mile, it was noted that the land was increasing in elevation, and at about a mile and a half, "heavy grade" was confronted. At the two-mile point, two fir trees were again used for recognition, one with a thickness of fourteen inches and the other ten inches. The 7-11 store at the top of the hill is in the same approximate location.

Just after the 2-mile point, the surveyors encountered a swamp. It measured 528 feet in length. At the 3-mile point, four fir trees were used to mark the location, two that were 12 inches in diameter, one at 24 inches and the other at 30 inches. At this point, the surveyors were close to where the Meridian Place Shopping Center is now located.

Between miles three and four, the land had a down slope, and another swamp was entered. At mile four, two trees were used to mark the location: one twenty-four-inch-diameter cedar and an eight-inch fir. After passing mile four, the team continued on south, still moving through a swamp and in dead timber. However, the ground was gradually rising. The five-mile point was marked by axing a symbol on three fir trees—twenty, thirty and ten inches in diameter.

Beyond the five-mile point, the group continued south for about a quarter mile and then turned east. That turn occurred around 160$^{th}$ Street in today's grid. Some open ground was then detected near the termination point and expanded for about a mile. The end point of the project was marked on two fir trees, one sixteen inches in diameter and the other twenty-four inches.

From this record, it is obvious that in the 1880s, South Hill was covered with a forest of large trees. The surveyors recorded fir trees up to 40 inches in diameter and 12-inch cottonwoods. A 40-inch-diameter tree would have a circumference of roughly 125 inches, and it would be about 200 feet tall. Moreover, there were swamps. So, the early settlers had a problem of clearing the land of both timber and water—not an easy task.

## The Kupfers and the Mosolfs

It appears the first permanent settlers on the Hill arrived during the late 1870s. Two families in particular should be considered South Hill pioneers: the Kupfers and the Mosolfs.

In 1877, Alois Kupfer established a homestead near what is now the intersection of Meridian Avenue and 112$^{th}$ Street (or 39$^{th}$ Avenue). It later became known as Willows Corner. Kupfer was born in Germany and arrived on the Hill after spending time in Montana, Utah, Oregon and eastern Washington. He bought his property through a real estate agent in Steilacoom. Not far from Kupfer's property was one of the two tribal camp sites on the Hill. Kupfer quickly became acquainted with the Puyallup Tribal members who stayed there, and it is said that the Native people gave their

# A Community History

Kupfer family, circa 1911. *Left to right*: (*sitting*) Fred Kupfer Sr., Alois Kupfer and Henry Kupfer; (*standing*) Tony Rauch, Lizzie Kupfer and Louis Kupfer. *Courtesy of South Hill Historical Society.*

The Kupfer home, circa the 1880s. *From left to right*: Fred Kupfer, his brother Louis, his sister Elizabeth, Jennie Evans, Henry Kupfer and Alois Kupfer. *Courtesy of Michael Kupfer.*

free consent for Kupfer to occupy the land. But Alois Kupfer encountered difficulties during his first winter there, and food was scarce. The Native people came to his aid, teaching him to cure food and sharing their dried clams and salmon. The story of the friendship between Kupfer and the Puyallup tribal members remains a part of the tribe's oral tradition.

Two years after Kupfer arrived, George Mosolf acquired land in the area of present-day Bradley Park. Mosolf came with his wife, Theresa, and two children from California. George was a native of West Prussia; he was born in 1837. Theresa was from Bohemia. George spent the first twenty years of his life in Germany and was a brewer by trade. He had immigrated to New York in 1857, lived for a while in Wisconsin and later went to California, arriving there around 1874. Theresa was born in 1850. She immigrated to Virginia but subsequently moved to California and worked as a housekeeper in San Francisco. It was there that the two met and were married. They later moved north to Washington Territory. By the time the 1889 census was recorded, they had five children in their home on South Hill: John (thirteen), George (twelve), Joseph (nine), Antoinie (seven) and Ennie (three).

Just how the Mosolfs traveled to South Hill is not known. Records show they used Steilacoom as their shopping center after they arrived. Such usage

Hop Kiln on George and Theresa Mosolf's property. *Courtesy of Ruth Anderson.*

would indicate that they probably reached their settlement using the old Military Road that connected Steilacoom and the Hill.

Some accounts put the Mosolfs' holdings at 180 acres, while other writings say it was 120 acres. Some reports say they homesteaded, while others declare the acreage was purchased from the Northern Pacific Railroad. Land records show they settled on about 100 acres. The place they chose was a dense forest on the hill above Puyallup, which was later known as Puyallup Heights. To locate it today, one has to move north from the South Hill Mall, on Meridian Avenue, toward the Puyallup Fair Grounds. As you crest the hill, look to the right, and in the distance, you will see the Sunset Apartments. These buildings are in the same approximate location as the farm.

Over the years, the family cleared the land. In keeping with George's early training, they initially grew hops for the brewing industry. For a while, this was a successful business. Later, they switched to berries and fruit. At times, the family was well known for their red raspberries and strawberries, as well as their crops of cherries.

Neither the Kupfers nor the Mosolfs came to the Northwest as Oregon Trail pioneers. It could be said that they represent a second wave of immigrants to settle the area. They did not travel by wagon or horseback; the railroads were in operation by the late 1870s, so that is undoubtedly how they arrived. As to why they settled on South Hill, the initial settlers had already taken all the prime land. This new group was forced to settle on less desirable tracts, like the rugged and heavily wooded sections like South Hill.

## Waves of Settlers

The settlement of South Hill happened in phases or waves. During the mid to late 1800s, for example, settlers usually arrived by wagon or on horseback. They were few in number. Some came in groups in the so-called wagon trains, while others came alone. These immigrants might be considered the first wave—or the original settlers on the Hill. The second wave came shortly after the railroads were established. These groups came in around the first decade of the twentieth century.

South Hill, Washington

## The Northern Pacific Railroad

Railroads had a significant influence on the use of land on South Hill; the impact of the railroads can be traced to federal actions in the 1860s and 1870s. During that period, transcontinental railroads were thought to be the way to connect the East and West Coasts for commerce and the movement of settlers to newly acquired lands. In 1869, the first line, named the Central Pacific/Union Pacific, was completed. It linked San Francisco and Chicago, but that track did not serve the Pacific Northwest.

In 1864, Congress passed legislation to bring railroading to the Northwest. It was signed into law by Abraham Lincoln. This act authorized a program to develop a railroad and telegraph line from Lake Superior to Puget Sound. The port on Puget Sound that was to be the terminal was Tacoma, not Seattle. The company that was formed to carry out this effort was named the Northern Pacific Railroad. The line was completed in 1883.

Paying for this proposed railroad was also a part of the law. It authorized, for example, that certain public lands along its right of could be granted to the Northern Pacific, which was then to sell this acreage to pay for construction costs. The grant was for every other square mile of land along the route, to a depth of either forty or eighty miles, depending on location. In Washington Territory, the depth was eighty miles. This created the so-called checkerboard pattern of allocations along the railroad's path.

The Northern Pacific's way through the Cascade Mountains was Stampede Pass. On the western side, the line passed through the present-day towns of Enumclaw, Buckley and Orting, and then it moved along the Puyallup River to Alderton, Puyallup and Tacoma. This route put the railroad just north of South Hill, between Orting and Puyallup. South Hill was, as a result, subject to the land allocations that were given to the railroad.

The Northern Pacific disposed of its lands on South Hill in a number of ways. Some parcels were sold to individual investors, but most were acquired by timber mogul Frederick Weyerhaeuser. A 1915 map, for example, shows that Weyerhaeuser, at that late date, still owned either all or parts of Sections 1, 15, 21, 23, 25, 27, 29, 31, 33 and 35—that's ten sections out of the thirty-six on South Hill, a total approaching one-third of the township. A section comprised one square mile, and the numbers illustrate the checkerboard pattern of the railroad's titles. As for sales to individuals, title abstracts can be found, even now, that illustrate land transfers.

Many South Hill land owners probably do not know the historical roots of their holdings, but many of their titles can be traced to the original grant awards that were given to the Northern Pacific Railroad.

# 2

# FARMERS

South Hill's agricultural roots run deep. Berries were the area's most famous crop. Before the berry vines were rooted, there were acres of hops. Hops were the earliest commercial agricultural venture on the Hill. Three local families accounted for most of the hop production: the Mosolfs, the Kupfers and the Muehlers. The Mosolfs were situated on the northern part of South Hill, in the general vicinity of present-day Bradley Lake. The Kupfer farm was nearby, close to what later became known as Willows Corner, at the present-day intersection of 112th Street and Meridian Avenue. The Kupfer home was located near the site of today's 39th Street and Meridian Avenue. The Muehler farm was farther south, near what is now Thun Field.

Carl F. Muehler, also known as "Swamp Muehler," settled on the southern end of South Hill, just to the east of present-day Thun Field. The intersection of 160th Street and 110th Avenue was be the approximate location of his farm. We know of this site because the Federal Land Office issued him a homestead certificate, no. 926, based on a patent dated March 1, 1879—it was for eighty acres. Mr. Muehler added to his holdings when he received a second homestead certificate, no. 2042, based on a patent dated July 20, 1886—it was for an additional eighty acres. According to these certificates, he apparently arrived on South Hill in the 1870s.

Mr. Muehler was a hop farmer, a native of Germany. He made a will on August 11, 1904, declaring that his age at that time was sixty-nine; therefore, he would have been born sometime in 1832. He was forty-seven years old when he first acquired property on South Hill, and he was fifty-

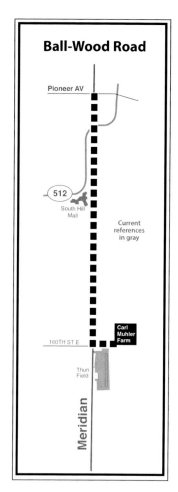

The Ball-Wood Road, starting at the Muehler ranch, gave Hill farmers access to the Puyallup market. *Courtesy of Jerry Bates and the South Hill Historical Society.*

four when he expanded his holdings. He and his wife, Louisa, had three children who were born in Germany (Agnes, Otto and "S") and one who was born in Washington (Albin). Carl Muehler died in 1912.

When the hop farm was first established, there was no road system on South Hill. The Muehlers' accessed the markets for their crops by using the trails on the inclines toward Orting. These trails also gave them access to the Puyallup River and to the transcontinental railroad. This lack of a transportation infrastructure continued to plague them and others until the creation of the Ball-Wood Road in the 1890s.

The importance of Ball-Wood Road can be appreciated by examining its original path. The road began just outside Puyallup and continued south and up the north side of South Hill before eventually ending at the Muehler farm. This road, the first planned one on South Hill, was built specifically along the center section lines of Township 19 until it reached a point around present-day 152$^{nd}$ Street. At that place, it moved east for about one-half mile to the Muehlers. That project made it possible for them to have market access through Puyallup. There is more on Ball-Wood Road—or as it would later be called, Meridian Avenue—in chapter 5.

Hops were grown on South Hill from the late 1800s through the early 1900s. This period generally parallels the time that the crop was cultivated elsewhere in the region.

While the end of the hop growing era can be pinpointed rather accurately because of an aphid infestation, the beginning of the era is more obscure. In the late 1860s and early 1870s, the regional breweries had become very concerned about the price of hops being imported from Europe. This ingredient, which is necessary for beer, was being tightly controlled and getting expensive. To counter this trend, someone managed to acquire some

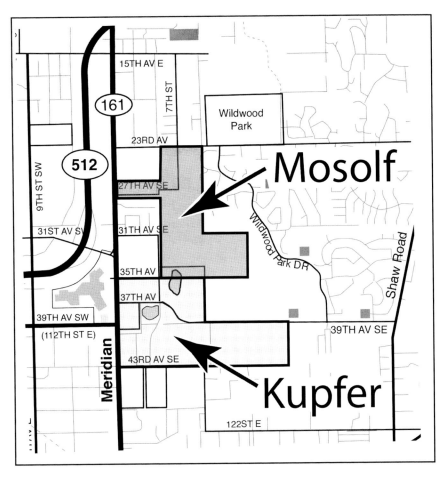

The approximate boundaries of the Kupfer and Mosolf properties over a current South Hill map. These boundaries are based on a 1915 Pierce County map that shows property ownership. *Courtesy of Jerry Bates and the South Hill Historical Society.*

hop seedlings. They were planted in the Puget Sound area and did well. As a result, a local industry was born.

The Kupfer family papers contain descriptions about how their hops were harvested. They emphasized the need for many workers for short periods of time. Local Native Americans were employed as much as possible, but most indigenous workers were recruited from the Frazier River Valley area of Canada.

Hops were grown on racks that were about twenty feet tall. These racks were lowered one at a time for picking. The seed cones were then stripped

The Kupfer farm hop harvest, circa 1900, on the east side of today's Meridian Avenue, across from the South Hill Mall. *Courtesy of Michael Kupfer.*

from the "bind." They were collected in a "hop basket," which held about twenty-five pounds. After four baskets were filled, they were dumped into a "hop box" and taken to a wagon. At that point, workers were credited with the weight they picked. Pickers were paid from one to five cents per pound. A daily wage was usually between eighty cents and one dollar per person.

## A Swedish Family

Dorothy Swalander Norris's roots on the Hill go back to 1897, when her grandfather, Rheinhold Swalander, bought property and settled on South Hill. Dorothy's grandfather and his brother, Carl, left Sweden in March 1883 and arrived in New York in April 1883. They traveled to Kansas, stayed for a couple of years and then moved on to Washington. Her grandfather rented property in Fife on the Puyallup Reservation. He and his young wife, who had also traveled from Sweden, had three daughters and one son. Their son, the oldest, died in the winter of 1890. The valley was flooded, and there was no way for the doctor to get to the house to treat the sick child. Thanks to the Puyallup Natives, the family managed to bring the doctor to their home by canoe, but it was too late; the boy had already died of appendicitis. The generous Natives even furnished clothes for the girls to wear for the funeral.

## A Community History

In 1897, Rheinhold purchased property on South Hill, no longer wanting to live in the valley with its floods. The land was located to the east of the Summit area and straddled today's Pipeline Road. Only one acre of the original eighty bought by Rheinhold is left today. The old farmhouse still stands on the remaining acre, which continues to be in the possession of the family.

Dorothy's colorful great-uncle, Carl, came from Sweden with her grandfather. He lived in a shack built of shakes and insulated with newspaper. He grew vegetables, had chickens, and sold his produce, as Dorothy remembers, on Vashon Island. Amazingly, he eventually earned enough to buy a house in Puyallup, which he leased out. Dorothy told an amusing story about him and his rental home. His renters were not paying the rent, so in order to get rid of them, he moved in upstairs and made enough noise to force them out.

Carl Swalander worked very hard, even with only one leg, having lost the other in a sawmill accident. "He was a real survivor," said Dorothy.

One interesting feature of the old Swalander farmhouse on South Hill is the huge Swedish whitebeam tree that was planted from a seed that had been mailed in an envelope from Sweden in 1897. The old tree still stands "but is starting to lean a bit," according to Dorothy.

The Swalander family home, located on the farm purchased by Rheinhold Swalander in 1897, is one of the oldest houses remaining on South Hill (picture taken in 2004). *Courtesy of South Hill Historical Society.*

# South Hill, Washington

## The Zimmermans

Louis and Mary Zimmerman arrived in Puyallup in October 1909. They came from Lake County, South Dakota, as part of the second wave of settlement on South Hill. Louis had been attracted to the Tacoma area as a result of his visit to the Alaska Yukon Fair in Seattle, at which time, Louis and his father, Fred, had toured the state.

The Zimmermans traveled to the Northwest by train. The Zimmerman party consisted of Louis and Mary, their five children, Louis's father, Fred Zimmerman, and two friends, Jim Blake and Bill Voight. Louis rented what was known as an emigrant freight car from the railroad company. In this car, he packed all the agricultural items and tools he thought he would need to operate a farm, and he brought along two draft horses.

On South Hill, the Zimmermans bought fifty acres near what is now the Woodbine Cemetery. Shortly after arriving, they started building a house. It was finished on Thanksgiving Day in 1910, and the family moved in.

Clearing the acreage on South Hill turned out to be a formidable task, as it was heavily wooded. In 1912, Louis had an accident while pulling stumps. His injuries essentially ended his ability to do heavy farming labor. Being unable to work, Louis searched for an alternative way to make a living. He decided to enter the chicken business. In 1916, Louis attended what was called the "Chicken School" at the Washington State Experimental Station in Puyallup. Using the knowledge he obtained in this course, he built three elongated chicken coops on his property. He used these to raise baby chicks. He kept mature chickens to produce eggs that were used by his family and sold to others. To finance the start of his new business, Louis sold his horses. He raised fryers and sold them for meat to local markets. At one time, the Zimmerman family was supplying chicken products to buyers in Tacoma, Seattle and as far away as New York. The Zimmermans maintained their chicken farm throughout the 1920s and 1930s. They also grew raspberries.

Around World War II, the chicken and berry businesses were phased out. Ray Zimmerman, the son of Louis and Mary, turned the farm into a stable and horse-riding ranch. He operated this business for many years. The farm was sold in 1989 and is now a housing project.

## Down Ball-Wood Road

Meridian Avenue, from today's South Hill Mall to the Paul Bunyan Rifle and Sportsman's Club, stretches south for about five miles. If we go back to over one hundred years ago, to 1915, and trace the road, we can learn about what the Hill was like. Ball-Wood Road, as Meridian Avenue was then known, was a muddy path more than a road, and it only stretched to around today's 160th Street. As for the population density at that time, land ownership can be used as an indicator. An atlas published by the Knoll's Company, dated May 1915, can be used to identify various proprietorships.

The first mile south of Puyallup along Ball-Wood Road had the most development. At that time, however, only ten landowners held registrations on the western side of the road. These were small farms, measuring, in general, about five or so acres. On the eastern side, there were only eight farms. The largest landowner along this first mile was Louis Kupfer, who held an eighty-acre farmstead.

Along the second mile, there was less congestion, with only three landowners on each side (around today's 128th Street). Mr. M.S. Edgerton was the largest property owner on the east side, possessing 320 acres, with one-half mile of it fronting Ball-Wood Road. On the west side, there was a tract for a housing development named the Half Dollar Berry Tract. It comprised 320 acres, but it was still undeveloped land. A second commercial holding was that of the Scandinavian American Bank, totaling 160 acres. These two plots together took up about three-quarters of the road's frontage. They were located near where the old Military Road (Naches Pass Trail) crossed Ball-Wood Road.

All of mile three on the west side was designated as school land. Of the entire 640 acre section, only two small plots were privately owned: one by F.L. Kupfer and the other by Orvis Powers. The eastern side was somewhat denser, with five small farms and two large holdings by the Weyerhaeuser Timber Company.

Mile four was dominated by the Weyerhaeuser Timber Company, which owned all but 40 acres on the west side. On the eastern flank, there were two landowners, Frank Hartman and Kee Harrison, who each held 160 acres. Their plots were located near today's Sunrise Village Shopping Center, where the Ball-Wood Road ended in 1915.

In the five mile zone, ownership on the west side was split between Joel Martin (160 acres) and the Story Timber Company. The eastern side was entirely owned by the Weyerhaeuser Timber Company.

This record shows that, in 1915, South Hill was very open. There was some development just south of Puyallup, but otherwise, there were few property owners.

## OLE AND EMILY GABRIELSON

On August 12, 1921, the Gabrielson family left Pocatello, Idaho, in a covered wagon (likely one of the last emigrant families to travel in this way), bound for South Hill. The family included Swedish-born Ole; his wife, Emily; and a six-week-old daughter, Margie. Ole and Emily had been married in Cascade County, Montana, the year before. Unlike earlier immigrants who used oxen, the Gabrielsons' wagon was pulled by two horses named Jake and Fly. Fly, a female, had a three-month-old colt with her. For the most part, the party first traveled on the old Oregon Trail and subsequently on the Naches Pass Trail. They did not go through Naches Pass but instead crossed the mountain through Snoqualmie Pass.

The family first went to Arlington and rested with a relative. Then, they continued the trip to South Hill. Diary records show that it took forty-three days to travel between Pocatello and Arlington. While records do not exist, it is estimated that it took them another five days to reach South Hill. So, the entire trip took about fifty days; it was about 850 miles or roughly 17 miles per day.

While the horses were able to make the entire trip, the colt did not. It was sold for five dollars on August 19 near Picaboo, Idaho.

The family apparently made the trip in fine shape. Mrs. Gabrielson later said, "Baby was 3 months old when we arrived…not a cold or anything else wrong, not even a diaper-rash."

The Gabrielsons were typical of the second wave of immigrants who settled South Hill. Ole and Emily Gabrielson owned a forty-acre farm in Section 21 of Township 19. In today's system, this holding would be on the south side of 152$^{nd}$ Street, near its intersection with 86$^{th}$ Avenue. Section 21 was originally part of a federal land grant that was awarded to the Northern Pacific Railroad for building a railway into the Puget Sound area. It was subsequently sold to the Weyerhaeuser Timber Company. After all the marketable timber had been removed, the land was transferred to the Weyerhaeuser Logged Off Land Company. It was from this latter organization that Mr. Gabrielson acquired the farm. The

In 1921, the Gabrielson family left Pocatello, Idaho, in a covered wagon, bound for South Hill. *Courtesy of Katie Bennett.*

address of the farm in 1927 was Puyallup, Washington, Route 2, Box 85. U.S. Post Office Route 2 served the residents of this part of South Hill. The Gabrielsons kept farm animals, such as cows and pigs, to provide food for the family. One of their cash crops was raspberries, which they sold in Puyallup.

On February 29, 1928, Ole Gabrielson visited the office of Pierce County treasurer J.E. Tallant to pay his annual tax bill. His tax bill for 1927 was $26.43. The land (forty acres) was valued at $280.00 and the house was valued at $125.00. He paid taxes on the total valuation of $405.00. The Pierce County tax levy for 1927 was divided into three parts: general state and county charges, a special school tax and a road districts tariff. The general state and county account included such things as the current expenses of running the state and county. For this general part, as expressed in levy terms, Mr. Gabrielson's tax bill was 35.27 mills. The special school district charge, District 82, added an additional 22.00 mills and the road district; District 3 added 10 mills, for a total of 67.42 mills. Thus, on the $405 value of his property, he was charged a tax of $27.24. However, a 3 percent discount was authorized since he paid before March 15, 1928, and that reduced his obligation by $0.81, to $26.43. In today's money, the same tax bill would be $348.75. The value of the land and buildings in the current market would be in the millions of dollars.

As for Ole and Emily, who were British subjects at the time of their move, they subsequently acquired U.S. citizenship. Ole Gabrielson died on May 8, 1965, and was buried in Woodbine Cemetery. Emily lived until 1997. Many of their children and grandchildren still live on South Hill.

# Gabe Gabrielson

Ole's brother, Gabriel Gabrielson ("Gabe"), also settled on the Hill. He acquired a forty-acre farm near present-day 146th Street and 86th Avenue. Significantly, Gabe kept a journal that gives some insight into this period.

As a farmer, Gabe kept a variety of livestock. Both chickens and cows were maintained for food for the family and for products that could be sold. Horses were held for farmwork since motorized farm tools were not affordable. Pierce County public records show that in 1943, Gabe owned two work horses, four milk cows, one bull and two heifers. The horses were used for work both on and off the farm. Over time, the family had several cows that they used for dairy products and as breeding stock. These creatures were not, however, just a dairy herd—they were practically family pets. They were given names; Boots, Mollie, Brindle, Patty and Pigie are mentioned in different accounts. Boots, for example, gave birth to a calf on February 1, 1935; again on February 21, 1936; and on January 17, 1937. Records of births from the other cows were similarly recorded. About every nine months, each cow produced a calf. Most calves were sold for veal when they weighed about 120 pounds. Each spring, Gabe faithfully "set" his poultry hens on eggs to hatch young chickens.

Plowing the land started in March. Potatoes were planted in May. Oats and clover were seeded in April and May. In the fall, around November, the pasture was seeded. Gabe also recorded the planting dates for important crops, including potatoes, corn and oats, and he recorded the dates of weather events, like snowfall.

In addition to farming, Hill residents also supplemented income by off-farm work. The McMillin Reservoir, for example (which was near today's 128th Street), was an employer of some importance in the 1930s. Gabe worked there from time to time, starting in the spring of 1936, and he undertook the following duties: cleaning, reservoir building, repairing woodstove pipes, blacksmithing, carpentry, repairing leaks on pipe line, sweeping and other tasks. It was also in the mid-1930s that the Federal

Works Progress Administration began a stimulus program, creating public works jobs during the Great Depression. Gabe Gabrielson participated in that effort and was assigned chores on the Hill, in Tacoma and as far away as Enumclaw.

As a laborer, Gabe worked, at times, for Pierce County. In August 1941, he was employed on the water pipeline at White River. In early 1942, he started work at the McMillin Reservoir on the Hill, where he stayed for several years. He died in May 1948 and was buried in Woodbine Cemetery.

## Barth Family

### *By Debbie Burtnett*

After Eunice Barth Gilliam died in 2007, her daughter Chris Gilliam Nimick discovered among her papers the manifest of the ship her ancestors landed in at Kaua'i on June 18, 1881. Several years after that, the family left the island for the Pacific Northwest. A family member's letters encouraged them to visit Orting in Washington Territory.

Fred Jr., Chris's grandfather, arrived to explore the area in 1888–1889, just as statehood was conferred on the territory, and he stayed to work as a carpenter. A year later, Fred Sr. and his wife, Margaretha, along with Fred Jr.'s siblings—Henry, William and Mary—arrived to live and farm in Orting.

Fred Jr. met a young woman named Magnaline Marie Kistenmacher in Puyallup; she worked in the Ma Bell telephone office on West Meeker Street. They were later married and lived in the Puyallup Valley, but they bought a house in the Bradley Park area from Theresa Mosolf, or "Old Mrs. Mosolf" as she was known then. On the death of Mrs. Mosolf, the family moved to the house on the Hill.

The twenty-acre family farm included a dairy herd. Fred Barth Jr. raised Holstein cows, which had milk that was lower in fat. Chris Nimick recalled milking the cows as a child and said that the taste of "cold, fresh milk" as an "amazingly wonderful thing."

The Barths enjoyed the "panoramic view of Mt. Rainier." Nimick said, "You could see the Olympics clearly and all the way to Tacoma….My grandfather watched the mountain and could 'predict' when rain and floods were coming." Life on the Barth farm was quiet. "I never remember the back door being locked," said Nimick.

Just before Fred Barth Jr. died in 1970, his tranquil place on the hill was interrupted by the noise of "heavy equipment on 512," Nimick recalled. As dozers cut into the Hill, her grandfather said, "They've found us. It's all over now." Then, in 1987, just as the area near her home was being cleared for the South Hill Mall, Magnaline Marie Barth passed away.

## The Van Pevenage Family

### By Debbie Burtnett

The Van Pevenage family once lived next door to the Barth family on South Hill. The Van Pevenages found their way from Belgium to South Hill by way of Missouri and Kansas. Three generations had settled on South Hill by the 1930s. "Staying together meant the family remained 'close knit,'" said Lee Van Pevenage, who is a member of the South Hill Historical Society. Lee's grandfather Emile Van Pevenage purchased property at the top of Meridian Avenue, a tract of seven acres that was lost to Highway 512 when it came through. Lee said:

> *An uncle, John, bought a home with seven acres on the west side of Meridian* [Avenue], *just four houses north of my grandparents. On the other side of Meridian* [Avenue], *right across from my grandparents, my Uncle Albert Van Pevenage owned a home and twenty acres, about where Home Depot is located today. When eminent domain took the grandparents' property, they moved next to Ninth and Ninety-Seventh* [Streets], *where my aunt lived on ten acres….My grandparents' property is where Target is located today.*

According to Lee, one didn't have to have a lot of money to buy farmland. His parents purchased a seven-acre farm on Andrian Road, now Seventy-Ninth Street, in 1955, and they remained there until 1963. His father bid on property on Eightieth Street, and he got the property for $3,000. "The problem was, my dad didn't have the money, and banks wouldn't lend him money for forty-five acres, so he went to his cousin, making a 'handshake deal.'" It was unfortunate that the "deal" was off with his cousin, which angered his father. So, another deal was struck; his father got twenty-five acres (or forty-nine lots), which was known as Cedar Crest Estates, and put in wiring, phones and similar infrastructure at a cost of $7,000, or approximately $138 per lot. He built homes there, including one for himself and a couple for other family members.

The lots in Van Estates were sold at a cost between $2,000 and $3,000, and they fronted Eightieth Avenue East. Lee shared several lessons he learned during these years. At the age of eleven, in 1955, he recognized the unity that his family "had and still [has]." He said, "We'd gather at Christmas… and other times.…We had a great family background." He also learned the value of his ancestors. "Had I taken the time to know my grandfather better, I should have talked to him more…recorded more." And, after an absence that spanned between 1968 and 1978, he returned to the Hill. "I couldn't believe the Hill when I came back. It still surprises me that we've put as much traffic as we have on Meridian [Avenue], without some foresight."

## God's Country

Art Foxford's family came west from Illinois in the summer of 1920. His mother's friend, who lived in Sumner, coaxed them to Washington, writing, "You've got to come out here; it's God's country." After his father lost his job, Art said, "[We] got on a train for Washington…with my infant older sister in a dresser drawer." They arrived in Sumner and set up temporary shelter on their friend's farm, which was located on today's Sumner High School athletic field. The Foxfords later bought property and built a cabin on South Hill. Their property was next to the Gabrielson farm, where the two families became very close. As pictures in Art's collection show, the Hill residents during these times were mostly living in humble cabins on a landscape of stumps. Timber from the Hill remains in the form of leftover trees, and many huge stumps were put to good use for heating, cooking and building.

## Growing Up in the Berry Fields

### *By Helen (Heil) Rohlman, April 14, 2007*

Our South Hill community was basically a rural agricultural area in the 1930s and 1940s. In the Woodland School area, we had four businesses: Howard Allen's Grocery off 112$^{th}$ Street and Cedar Road (80$^{th}$ Avenue East);

the Woodland Grocery, which was owned by E.C. Allen (the father of Ted and Harry) on the corner of Woodland Avenue and Knapp Road (104th Street East); and along Fruitland Avenue, we had Gilliland's Grocery and "Gut" Johnson's Tallow Works—boy, did it stink.

The young people, wanting money for new school clothes, were destined to follow the crops, as no child labor laws were in effect at that time. We started the season picking strawberries for Lester and Faye Goelzer, Bill's parents. They were wonderful people to work for. From my recollection, some of the hired pickers were Patty (Van Horn) Goelzer and her mother, Mildred; some of the Parks girls, Carol Parks and Joan (Parks) Vosler; Bob Crabb; and the Heil girls, Mildred Dobbs and Helen Rohlman, and their mother, Helena. The mothers worked daily with their children to guarantee their "bonuses," which were given as incentives to work the whole season.

Then the raspberry season started, and South Hill had few large raspberry fields to be harvested, so Cliff Miller and his wife, Hazel Whitford Miller, would pick up a bunch of kids in the Fruitland and Woodland areas in a big berry truck, take us to the fields and return us home in the afternoon. Some names I remember are Barbara Huff; the Strandley girls, Lillian, Betty and Eleanor; Joan (Parks) Vosler and her sister, Carol; Patty (Van Horn) Goelzer; several Templin brothers; Julia and Lynn Williams; Ronald Crabtree; and the Heil girls again. Everyone loved picking for NIF and Hazel. They were always fair, not mean-spirited, had lots of drinking water in the berry shed, paid a reasonable bonus at season's end—and the absolute best incentive of all was a trip to NIF and Hazel's Clear Lake cabin for a few exciting days at the lake.

Blackberries, beans and bulb jobs were also available, but most families only had one vehicle, and the fathers generally used them to go to work. So, the kids were often relegated to finding jobs closer to home.

There was little leisure time left during our summer vacation after the berry picking season, but it was always exciting to take the Woodland bus to Tacoma to select our school clothes for the coming year.

## Farming Evolves

In the early days on South Hill, the farms comprised large tracts; some were as big as 360 acres, or a full section in the platting grid system. But by the 1940s and 1950s, most of these earlier areas had been subdivided so many times that a typical parcel might have comprised about forty acres. By the mid-century, most farms were small family operations.

The farms on the Hill in the 1940s and 1950s might have comprised forty acres, like Glaser farm, shown here. *Courtesy of Don and Mary Glaser.*

## Memories of Rhubarb

### *By Jerry Bates*

South Hill doesn't necessarily come to mind when thinking about rhubarb. The valley areas around Puyallup and Sumner have been and continue to be the leading producers of rhubarb in the United States, but did the farmers of old South Hill ever get involved with this crop commercially?

Don Glaser and Bill Goelzer, lifelong residents of the hill, can easily remember when small farms dominated the lives of those who lived here, long before shopping malls and housing developments moved into the region. They both recall a time when commercial rhubarb farming did exist on South Hill.

Glaser recalled a period during his childhood, from about 1935 to 1943, when his grandfather owned and operated a rhubarb farming business on property that was next to where Don's family lived. Don's grandfather Joe Glaser farmed on forty acres that were located on the corner of today's 144th Street East and 122nd Avenue East (Glaser Road). The ranch had 150 fruit trees and raspberry fields in addition to the ten to fifteen acres of rhubarb. The present-day pond that can be seen from 144th Street was, back then, drained by a long ditch the Glasers dug across their property, exposing rich peat soil where the rhubarb was planted.

In addition to the rhubarb fields, five rhubarb hothouses were built on the property. The hothouses were windowless structures approximately fifteen by eighty feet with walls that were low to the ground and roofs that peaked at around ten feet. The rhubarb started out growing in the field for two summers before it was ready for the hot house. Don remembers the hard work that was involved in harvesting the rhubarb root balls. A single-blade, horse-drawn plow would turn the roots up. Then Don, as a child among the farmhands, would lift the heavy root balls into a waiting wagon. The roots would be planted in the hothouse. After two months, they were ready to be harvested. The hothouse was heated during the winter growing months, using fifty-five-gallon oil drums that had been made into wood stoves. The result of all this effort was hothouse rhubarb, which was much superior to the field-grown variety. Hothouse rhubarb has a 50-percent-greater sugar level and is more tender, making for better pies and preserves. Don and the Glaser family members would harvest the ripe rhubarb using a long sharp knife; one swipe would cut off the root and a second would remove the leaves.

Don's grandfather sold the ranch and retired from farming between 1948 and 1949.

# 3
# NEIGHBORHOODS

South Hill has long been a community of neighborhoods. While today's neighborhoods go by names like Crystal Ridge, Manorwood and Sunrise, the neighborhoods of earlier times had names like Willows, Firgrove, Puyallup Heights, Woodland and Rabbit Farms. While none of these place names were legal designations, they had great significance to the people who lived in these places.

## Woodland

The Woodland neighborhood can roughly be defined as the area between 112th and 96th Streets and between 78th Avenue and Canyon Road. It is the northwest sector of South Hill and was one of the first spots on the Hill to be settled.

Several landmarks bear the Woodland name. Woodland Avenue connects the Hill with flatlands. Woodland School is located on 112th Street, near Fruitland Avenue. Established in 1884, this was one of the first educational establishments on South Hill, and it sits on land that was donated by Puyallup pioneer legend Ezra Meeker.

The first region of the Hill to be subjected to a planned increase in density was the Woodland community. It was in September 1890 that Stephen Nolan and his wife, Helen, along with Michael Shea and his wife, Eva, platted the Hill's first high-concentration development. It was named the Shea and Noland's Five Acre Tracts. Five-acre lots may not seem high-density now, but at the time, it was very close-knit thinking. The plan included about forty five-acre lots or roughly two hundred acres. The project bordered both sides of present-day Woodland Avenue, north of 112th Street.

The second high-density undertaking was started in 1891 and was located just to the east of the Shea and Noland venture. It was platted by the Tacoma & Puyallup Railroad Company and named Fruitland. The community comprised around thirty 4-acre lots or 120 acres. This property also included the Woodland School site, which had been there since 1885.

Thus, while most of South Hill's initial land usage started as farms of various sizes, high-density housing areas also began developing early. Initially, such development was not significant, but eventually, it forced out large-scale agricultural ventures in those neighborhoods.

Around 1908, one of the first of the large expansions, Puyallup Fruit and Garden Tracts, was initiated. It straddled Sections 4 and 5 of Township 19 and bordered the southern line of the Puyallup city limits. Later, it was part of the Woodland area. The project consisted of seventy-two lots, with a total area of one-half section, or 320 acres. Sixteen of the lots were two and one-half acres in size; the rest comprised five acres.

One of the interesting things about this neighborhood was the naming of its streets. In keeping with the overall theme, several routes, for example, were named for fruits and vegetables. There was an east–west path across the northern top of the project, bordering the Puyallup city line, known as Grape Street. A thoroughfare called Pear Street was built across the southern edge. North–south throughways were constructed between each of the equal areas of the project. Each went completely through the development. In keeping with the project theme, the most-western route was called Walnut Avenue. The most-eastern thoroughfare was called Apple Way. The center lane was called Cherry Street. Those early streets have since been renamed. Grape Street is now 96th Street East, and Pear Street is 104th Street East. The north–south streets have also been redefined. Walnut Avenue is now 82nd Avenue East; Cherry Street is 86th Avenue East; and Apple Way is 90th Avenue East.

The original name, Puyallup Fruit and Garden Tracts, has virtually disappeared as a community indicator. It is more generally known as the Woodland area, if it is recognized at all.

The writings of Ruth Lillian Sharpe Knoll provide some insight as to what Woodland was like in the period between 1907 and 1925. Her family

# A Community History

A typical road construction crew for early South Hill Roads, shown here on Woodland Road circa 1900. *Courtesy of Dorothy Norris.*

bought property in Woodland in 1907 and moved onto the Hill in 1910. They acquired ten acres from Mike Shea, part of the so-called Shea and Noland Five Acre Tracts development. The Sharpe family came from Buffalo, New York. They arrived in Tacoma in 1905. Ruth said that, in the early 1900s, the Woodland area was "a very desolate place." Initially, electricity was unknown in the region. Kerosene lamps were used for lighting. Each family had to dig their own well for water, and most water sources would usually go dry during the summers. Only a few natural springs existed, and at times, they provided water to entire communities.

In 1910, the Woodland area still had old-growth timber. Some logging had been done, and many acres were covered with stumps and rubble from that work. Those who had moved to the Hill had to clear the land before a house could be built or a garden could be planted, but there were wild berries and wildflowers that could be gathered. Very few roads existed, and those that did were little more than paths. These paths were not paved, and at times, deep mud made travel difficult.

The Sharpe family selected property that bordered present-day 104th Street. At that time, the pathway was actually a railed streetcar line, which gave them easy access to Tacoma. (There is more information on this in chapter 4.)

The Woodland School was the social focus during this period. Community activities and neighborhood planning was the work of the Woodland Improvement Club, in cooperation with the county and others. The club lobbied to get water piped into the area and for other improvements, such as the construction of better roads. Puget Power brought electricity to the area in 1925.

## South Hill, Washington

# Puyallup Heights

Puyallup Heights was a common designation in early South Hill history, as the hillside and plateau area above the city of Puyallup was generally called Puyallup Heights. The designation first appeared in the 1890s and early 1900s. Geographically, it was an area at the top of the Hill, just above the city of Puyallup, that encompassed the area that now comprises the South Hill Mall, Willows Corner and the areas to the south, near present-day 128th Street.

After about 1900, more dense concentrations of housing began to appear in the Puyallup Heights neighborhood. This area was not densely populated by today's standards, but it was comparatively compact at the time. In the beginning, there was no extensive or fast change, but there was a movement, nevertheless.

# Rabbit Farms

Over the years, real estate on South Hill has been acquired, developed and sold in a variety of ways. One of the more interesting efforts was an attempt during the Great Depression to create a community known as Rabbit Farms. The intent was to divide a large geographical area into home lots, with each owner raising rabbits in commercial numbers, thereby creating an industry. Each dwelling lot would have a rabbitry, and breeding animals would be provided for the owners. They were to primarily produce rabbit fur, but they were also used to produce food and fertilizer. Rabbit meat was a growing market then and was competing with chicken. The approach was successfully promoted during the 1930s and 1940s. Many of today's Rabbit Farms residents are proud to claim lineage to this scheme. The development consisted of small, cheaply built houses on adjacent lots, each with rabbit hutches. The site was designed to be a communal effort to raise rabbits commercially. The idea was to attract residents who would pool together their incomes and raise rabbits during the hard times.

The records of Pierce County are not helpful in locating the old development. The effort was never registered, but it was real. Many period maps show its outline, and some even have individual lots identified. The concept was widely announced in newspaper advertisements of the time and was, therefore, a well-known activity. A present-day landmark close to the old Rabbit Farms area is the Mel Korum Family YMCA. The project was about two blocks east of the current YMCA, along 110th and 111th Avenues (then Fir and Cedar Streets), and then west–east on 122nd Street (then Main Street). Generally, the project was one lot deep along both avenues. Along 122nd Street, the depth varied as it moved from west to east, but it was generally one lot wide on both sides to about 120th Avenue. The project did not extend as far as Shaw Road.

The size of the proposed venture varied over time. In the 1930s, some six hundred acres was announced as the goal, but that number was never achieved. Analyses of maps suggest that about ninety-five building lots were finally used. As they were generally plotted at 2.5 acres, the final project was, therefore, about 250.0 acres.

Why was it thought that raising rabbits could be a viable activity? Natural fur was in fashion at the time, and rabbit fur could be dyed to resemble pelts of exotic animals. (This was before the introduction of synthetic fibers.) During the same period, the federal government was also expanding its research into using rabbit fur. Moreover, there were other fur farms in western Washington, and a number of professional associations existed to represent marketing on a national basis.

The Rabbit Farms venture succeeded in selling real estate but not in the creation of an industry. While many people were attracted to the development because of the economic conditions of the 1930s, they were never able to produce enough rabbits to make it economically viable. Many of the old timers from that period also speak of a virus that hit the farms in the early 1940s. Most farmers never recovered. A few switched to raising chickens. And by the 1950s, economic times had changed, and the market for fur had diminished.

The Rabbit Farms area was later known as the Highlands in the 1960s and 1970s. Even today, there are specific places that incorporate Highlands into their names.

## Landmarks

Amid the farms and neighborhoods of the Hill, several landmarks figure prominently in the memories of those who grew up when South Hill was a rural place. Some of these landmarks still exist.

## Floyd's Hill

Floyd's Hill is located at the eastern end of Rabbit Farms. Most of 122nd Street, which moves west to east through Rabbit Farms, is flat, but at the eastern end of the street, around present-day 120th Avenue, there is a significant change in the landscape. On the south side, there is a considerable rise of about a hundred feet—that's Floyd's Hill.

Floyds' Hill was so named because of the several families who lived there: Temple and Frank Floyd resided near its top, and Don Floyd's family lived near the foot of the hill. In the 1960s, this area was relatively undeveloped, so the location was somewhat isolated. It was a perfect place for Rabbit Farm youngsters to congregate and play with the Floyd children and others. In the winter, it was especially attractive during snowfalls, as it was a great place to go sledding.

The name Floyd's Hill cannot be found on any map and does not exist in most common data bases, but the place is real in the minds of many of the older residents on South Hill, especially those who grew up in Rabbit Farms.

## The Duck Pond

This was a large natural pool located at the present-day intersection of 122nd Avenue and 152nd Street. Pope Elementary School now sits on the site. The small lake was filled in to build the school. Do you ever wonder why 152nd Street curves to the south just before 122nd Avenue? At one time, the road went around the duck pond.

## Massie's Pond

This is another natural lake that was named after the Massie family. It is located on modern 152nd Street, near Mystic Falls Water Gardens & Nursery (Tom's Nursery). Older residents recall it being three pools called "big," "middle" and "little." Local old timers remember skating there during the winter months. Others recall that it was a good fishing hole. Parts of this water hole are still visible, and what is left of the Big Pond can still be seen from 152nd Street. It was a well-known destination for young people during the 1940s and 1950s, and everyone knew its location.

# A Community History

## *Starkel's Pond*

This pond is no longer visible. It was directly behind the present-day Church of Jesus Christ of Latter-Day Saints just off Ninety-Fourth Avenue, and it was named for the nearby Starkel family. Because of the extensive development of parks and trails in this area, only some "wetlands" remain in this once-popular destination.

## *The Potato Patch*

During one growing season, probably in the 1940s, a landowner just off today's 122$^{nd}$ Avenue planted a field of potatoes around the present-day entrance of the Sunrise development (156$^{th}$ Street). Apparently, they were not harvested thoroughly because year after year, a spotty crop of potatoes returned. They were, in effect, growing wild. Many of the local youngsters who saw this unclaimed bounty used the field as a place to gather and party. Potatoes would be dug up, fires would be built and potato roasting would commence. It was a destination for many years until the open field gradually became covered with brush.

## *The Fir Thicket*

Almost adjacent to the potato patch, across what is now 122$^{nd}$ Avenue, was the fir thicket. It was an area of big fir trees that were growing in a clump; this created a type of natural park. It was a well-known location and a popular directional marker, e.g., "meet me by the fir thicket." This area is now part of the Springfield Estates community.

## *Cedar Swamp and Sand Hill*

Cedar Swamp is—or was—located on the western side of South Hill, between Meridian Avenue and Canyon Road. Geographically, it is a large area; it's about four miles long and generally oriented from north to south. The width of Cedar Swamp varies depending on where the measurements are made. And it must be noted that Cedar Swamp, having been generally drained, is not what it once was.

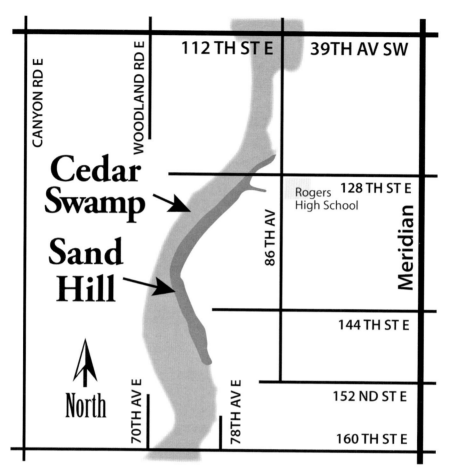

Cedar Swamp was located on the western side of South Hill, between Meridian Avenue and Canyon Road. *Courtesy of Jerry Bates and the South Hill Historical Society.*

To get an idea of its location, imagine driving west on 160th Street, from Meridian Avenue toward Canyon Road. At first, you are on generally level ground, but after passing by 78th Avenue, you start down a rather steep hill. The downhill grade continues for about a quarter mile, and you then ascend an equally steep hill, eventually intersecting Woodland Avenue. You have just crossed through Cedar Swamp near its southern end. You can also imagine taking a drive on 128th Street; starting at Rogers High School and traveling west, you immediately encounter a very steep downgrade. It also has a length of about a quarter mile. Continuing on, you enter an upgrade that takes you out of the dip and to the top of a hill. You have now crossed Cedar Swamp near its northern end. And if you search for a crossing between 128th Street and 160th Street, you will find that there isn't one.

To the early settlers, this was a formidable east–west obstacle. There were very few homes in the hollow, and there were no roads. Wild animals abounded, including bear and coyotes. It was a collection point for water runoff from the higher hills on both sides. At one time, it had been heavily wooded but was logged off early. Dorothy Norris (Swalander), who grew up in the 1930s next to the swamp, remembered her father using the area to pasture dairy cattle. The family generated some cash by selling cream. The raw milk was fed to the farm's calves and pigs. Bonnie Starkel (Nicolet) also grew up near the swamp and recalled that, at one time, her husband, Dave Starkel, and others herded cattle on horseback into the swamp.

So, if this is Cedar Swamp, where is Sand Hill? Anyone who has tried to dig a hole on South Hill knows that the soil is primarily glacial till—that is, mostly rocks. But it turns out that the retreating glacier that formed South Hill left numerous deposits of sand along the eastern slopes of Cedar Swamp. So, from a little north of Rogers High School to about where the electric transmission lines cross Cedar Swamp, there are many deposits of sand. The early settlers called this area Sand Hill.

## *Willows Corner*

The T-bone point where present-day Thirty-Ninth Street and Meridian Avenue come together was once recognized as Kupfer's Corner. Later, it was called Willows Corner. Today, it is known as the South Hill Mall and Willows Shopping Center. During the 1920s and 1930s, it was a destination for many people of Pierce County.

As early as 1915, several members of the Kupfer family owned land on the east side of Meridian Avenue, extending both north and south from the intersection, totaling over 240 acres. By the 1920s, the corner had a grocery store, a gas station and other commercial endeavors. Over time, the corner became known as Willows Corner due to a number of very large willow trees that dominated the landscape. The trees were located near the intersection of present-day Meridian Avenue and Thirty-Ninth Street. The reference to the trees made giving directions easier when speaking to people who did not know the Hill. Then, in 1939, a businessman named Al Delano bought most of the land around the intersection and maintained the "Willows Corner" designation.

Willows Corner in the early 1940s. The T formed where present-day Thirty-Ninth Avenue E and Meridian Avenue join at South Hill Mall. *Courtesy of South Hill Historical Society.*

During the prohibition period of the 1920s and 1930s, the Willows Dance Hall, just west of Willows Corner, was very popular. *Courtesy of John Potter.*

## A Community History

Willow trees were not limited to one location. They were scattered all around the local area, on both sides of Meridian Avenue and Thirty-Ninth Street, which was known for many years as Airport Road. Longtime Willows Corner resident Bill Goelzer, for example, remembered making whistles from the willows growing along the road while waiting for the school bus as a youngster.

During the 1920s and 1930s, one of the businesses operating in the area was the Willows Dance Hall. It was located on Thirty-Ninth Street, about where the U.S. Bank building is now located, just west of the intersection. This dance hall was very popular. Live music was always on the program, and a variety of local and regional bands played there. Advertisements in the local newspapers of the time declare that the admission price was seventy-five cents for gentlemen and twenty-five cents for ladies. It was reportedly a particularly popular location during the Prohibition era. The Willows Dance

A January 1972 aerial view of the Willows Corner neighborhood, including Willows Lumber in the bottom left corner and the former Willows Tavern, then known as the "Flea Mart," on the southwest corner of 112th and Meridian Avenue. This photograph was ordered by Puget Sound National Bank. *Courtesy of Tacoma Public Library, Richards Studio Collection, D161273-8.*

The construction of the Willows Shopping Center at 112th and Meridian Avenue was nearly complete when this aerial photograph was taken for Collison Realty on April 3, 1973. The ten-acre shopping center opened in May 1973 with a Piggly Wiggly supermarket, a State Farm Insurance office and a Sunrise Brokers office. Pay N Save and Puget Sound National Bank opened locations at Willows Shopping Center during the summer of 1973. Progress on State Route 512 is evident in this photograph to the northwest. *Courtesy of Tacoma Public Library, Richards Studio Collection, D163161-9.*

Hall experienced several catastrophic events during its time in business. During one winter in the 1930s, the roof caved in due to heavy snow. Finally, in the 1940s, it caught fire and completely burned down. It was never rebuilt. Today, there is no evidence of the dance hall.

Al Delano increased his holdings in 1944 to include acreage across Meridian Avenue. At that time, there were only a few homes and businesses close by. Mr. Delano promoted the Willows name at every opportunity. At the time of Mr. Delano's purchase, there was a tavern, a grocery store and an automobile service station on the property. During the next two decades, he developed a rather large commercial center. By 1957, the businesses included a barbershop, a food store, a tavern, a café, a lumber company and a trailer court. During this period, the

Willows was considered a center of economic development in central and eastern Pierce County. It was said to be the transportation hub for Hill people who were working in and around Tacoma and for those who were coming through the area to visit places like Mount Rainier. This was a continuation of the pattern set by World War II employment, when the local people supported the war effort at jobs primarily in the tide flats. The Willows Shopping Center on this corner was built in 1973. The name Willows has stuck, and many contemporary local businesses use it as part of their business names.

## Historic Homes

Are there historic homes on South Hill? While most houses on the Hill were built in the last forty years, there are a handful of older homes that remain.

### *The Parks House*

At the corner of 128th Street and 94th Avenue East is a home that was constructed entirely of logs (it's now covered with siding). Harold R. Parks built the structure in 1938 using locally logged timber. It is one of only a few houses on South Hill that is made entirely of indigenous forest products and has been in continuous use as a home since it was built. Moreover, this dwelling borders the Natches Pass Trail and is a part of the Pierce County Heritage Corridor.

### *The Swalander House*

This was one of the earliest homesteads on South Hill. In 1895, Oscar Swalander built it as a clapboard cottage. It has been in the family ever since and is located near 116th Street and 86th Avenue East. The Swalanders came from Sweden, and on this property, in addition to building a house, they planted the seeds from an Oxel tree at their home in Europe. That tree is now over one hundred years old.

## *The Lester House*

Built in 1914, the Lester House is located at 127th Street and 66th Avenue East. It was the first dwelling on the Hill to be declared historic by the South Hill Historical Society. Presently owned by Ralph and Yvonne Thorpe, the house was acquired from Rose Lester, the daughter of the builder. The house was moved from its previous location in the same neighborhood in the late 1990s.

## *The Arneson House*

Mr. Arneson and his three sons built this residence between 1911 and 1914. It is located near 102nd Avenue and 94th Avenue East. The land was actually acquired in 1908, but it was a "stump farm," and it took several years of grubbing to get the land cleared for other uses. This dwelling has been used both as a private residence and a business center. Since 1986, Robert and Lynne Daugherty have owned the house, which they maintain as a private residence.

## *The Zimmerman House*

This structure was built in 1910 and is located near 24th Avenue and 5th Street Southwest. Originally, the property encompassed some fifty acres and was operated as a farm. It has been said that the house is a smaller version of a previous Zimmerman home in South Dakota. It has changed hands a number of times over the years and is presently owned by Jessica Reich, who maintains it as a private residence.

# 4
# SCHOOLS

The educational needs of South Hill residents are served by the Puyallup School District, but this arrangement has only existed since the early 1950s. Before that, the Hill had a few locally designated rural schools, including the Firgrove, Woodland and Puyallup Heights Schools.

## Woodland School

Woodland School was established in 1884 in a cabin on Doc Breckon's homestead, land that previously belonged to pioneer Ezra Meeker. Known at first as Breckon School, the school was a simple cabin, and it had a student body of eight: Frank and Bill Breckon; Lena and Fred Kupfer; John and George Mosolf; and Maggie and George Hill. The first teacher, Maggie Wickersham, failed her teaching examination and vacated her teaching post after about two months. The second teacher was sixteen-year-old Lena Gano, who walked six miles from Clover Creek to get to the school.

Eventually, a one-room frame building replaced Doc Breckon's cabin as the schoolhouse. As more families moved into the Woodland neighborhood—around 1904 or 1905—a larger two-story school building was built on the old Breckon property. This building was named Woodland School. Then, during the Great Depression, in 1932, an even larger building was erected by the Works Progress Administration on the same grounds.

A student publication just after World War II offers insights on life in Woodland at the time. During the 1945–1946 school year, Woodland School published a newsletter called the *Woodland Flash*. It was declared to be the official school gazette, with a purpose stated as follows: "This [is] a school paper published monthly by the pupils of the $8^{th}$ grade in our school. It is used to teach the use of English, the art of spelling and penmanship. It also helps in the teaching of Arithmetic and business forms. THE PAPER DOES NOT PERMIT THE PUPIL TO NEGLECT THEIR REGULAR STUDIES." The newspaper was supported by local businesses, as a number of advertisements were scattered throughout the publication.

The February 1946 issue of the *Woodland Flash* comprised sixteen pages. It was published in mimeograph form on eight-and-a-half-by-fourteen-inch paper. In it, the staff wrote an editorial focusing on the lessons that they said should be learned from the lives of George Washington and Abraham Lincoln, whose birthdays were being celebrated during the month. The students noted, "[From George Washington,] we should learn the lesson of being truthful and honest and persevere in the right regardless of pending defeat.…[And from Lincoln,] we should learn the lesson that, no matter what our station is in life, perseverance, schooling, and decisiveness will overcome any obstacle in the way of our success." Since this edition was published at the end of World War II, a number of war items were presented. On several pages, readers were admonished to "Buy More Victory Bonds." This subject was considered so important that a chart was shown with a list of students' "January Bond and Stamp Sales," totaling $50.65. One advertisement declared, "TIRE RATIONING IS OVER. See us for new tires." One article explained that butter was still rationed.

It was reported that, during January 1946, the eighth grade hosted a visitor to the school. Captain James Repp Jr., formerly of the U.S. Army Air Corps, had lunch with the students and, afterward, gave a talk about his travels during the war. He was still in uniform but declined to discuss the meaning of the rows of ribbons he was wearing. He more willingly described the characteristics of the people he had seen during his tour of duty in the southwest Pacific for the class. He focused on the lives of people in the Philippines and other Pacific Islands. The boys in the class seemed to be particularly impressed with the fact that the women in those cultures did most of the manual labor. One boy was heard to say, "Gee, I'm going to live down there."

# A Community History

Woodland School, at that time, consisted of eight grades. Each class entered a report in the newsletter. They ranged, for example, from a description of the study of Eskimos by the first and fourth grades to the review of geography by the sixth, seventh and eighth grades.

Woodland School joined the Puyallup School District in 1957. While the 1932 Woodland School building was demolished in the early 1990s, the present-day building at $112^{th}$ Street and Fruitland Avenue sits on the same property where eight students first attended classes in the cabin on Doc Breckon's homestead in 1884.

---

### Grade School Days

*By Joan Parks Vosler*

The chill of the foggy September mornings greeted us as we stepped out the door to head down past the old cedar tree, which we called the cow shade tree, on our two-and-one-half-mile trek to Woodland School. An old lane that had been used to skid logs ran along the fence of the cow pasture, but we soon entered the trail through the woods, which curved and twisted its way to the gravel road. Addie, our Great Dane, always led the way. He never allowed us to pass him. He took his duties seriously. Many nights, we heard Dr. Oboe and his hounds camped at the sand pit, chasing coyotes by the light of the moon. Their sounds permeated the night and sent the hair standing on your neck. Addie knew what lurked about us, and he was our protector. Once we were out on the gravel road where there were some houses, he would leave us and return home.

That trail through the woods holds many memories, among them spiderwebs outlined by the morning dew. In the winter, snow weighed down the branches, and they blocked our way until our older brother shook them so we could continue on the trail single file. In the spring, we saw Johnnie jump-ups, trilliums, ginger leaves, wild currants in bloom, dogwoods, deer tongue, Indian paint brushes, tiger lilies, bleeding hearts and moss turning fallen limbs and logs into peculiar shapes. There were also green tree frogs, rabbits, birds, squirrels and croaking frogs, which I was told if I picked one up, I would get warts. Our mother had many bouquets of wildflowers that we picked on our way home. Douglas firs, cedars, graceful hemlocks, alders and vine maples lined the path we had worn through the woods. When we got to the gravel road, we would meet other kids who were on their way to school. Sometimes, we waited for them, and other times, we had to run to catch up.

Fifteen minutes before classes started, the school bell rang. It did not take long for everyone to sprint to the school yard so we could be lined up to march into class. On the way home, the sun would get warmer and warmer until those jackets and coats, much needed in the morning, would come off quickly. Following the pipeline road, we would always have Mount Rainier in view. We pretended we were hiking all the way to the mountain, which, in our imagination, became a huge ice cream cone. When we became tired of walking, we often trotted for a while, then walked some more. Then we did a short sprint and walked some more. It was always fun to come to a hill that we could run down with our slickers held high to catch the wind like a sail. When we arrived at the trail, Addie was always waiting for us, and we could hear our mother calling, "Yoo-hoo, yoo-hoo." We would answer in kind so she would know all was well.

I remember those days because they were filled with learning and adventure, most of the adventure provided by ourselves. The childhood friendships have remained all these years. The back twenty acres behind us is now a housing development, and a school bus takes the children to school. The adventures along the way to and from school are gone with our halcyon days.

## FIRGROVE SCHOOL

The Firgrove School District, located in the Firgrove neighborhood on the Hill, was established in the 1890s. The original school was made possible through the efforts of John Joseph Patzner. Patzner and his wife, Florence, moved from Michigan to Washington State in 1891. At first, they lived in Cle Elum, where Patzner worked in timber, cutting for mine construction. Then they moved across the Cascades and settled on an eighty-acre parcel on South Hill. Not long afterward, the Patzners arrived and purchased land from the original holdings of the Northern Pacific Railroad, and they donated land for a new school. The Firgrove School, as it was named, was built in 1895. It was originally a one-room wooden-frame building located on present-day 136th Street East, then known as Patzner Road, situated on a knoll about one-half mile east of Ball-Wood Road (now known as Meridian Avenue East).

Margaret Deagan was the teacher from 1908 to 1911. She wrote that some of the early family names of students included Fulliger, Patzner and Chadwick. Ms. Deagan was paid thirty-three dollars a month during her first year of teaching. She earned a three-dollar-per-month raise in years two and three. She was also the school janitor.

The original Firgrove School had a single entrance into a vestibule where the children kept their lunch buckets, which were usually "five-pound lard pails or square tobacco tins." It was also a place where their coats and books were stored during the day. There was a water pump in the passage, and the children all drank from a long-handled tin dipper, which hung alongside a pail of fresh water. In the classroom, there were three large blackboards, one on each side of the room and one in the front. The room was heated by a large air-tight wood-burning heater with a heavy zinc guard around the back and sides. The guard prevented the students from brushing against the hot stove.

Classes began at 9:00 a.m., and the daily activities closed at 4:00 p.m. Sessions were started when the teacher rang a large handbell. The school district provided chalk for use on the blackboards and firewood for the stove. Students provided their own books, paper, pencils and slates.

Ms. Deagan rode a horse to work each day. The school district provided a shed to house it while she was occupied. There were no automobiles on the roads during her tenure at Firgrove, and the nearest house was located at Kupfer's Corner, about one and one-half miles to the north. (In present-day terms, that would be the intersection of Meridian Avenue and 39th Street.)

Student interaction was fondly remembered. Ms. Deagan did not recall ever having trouble with students smoking, stealing, fighting or causing problems. She noted that some stayed after hours to ask questions about difficult subject matters, and in times of severe weather, they would bring their sleds to school and happily slide down the hill from the school.

As time passed, the community's educational needs increased and outgrew the original one-room school, but there was no room to expand. Four decades after the original Firgrove School was built on Patzner's land donation, John Joseph Patzner was the chair of the Firgrove School Board.

Seeing the need for a new school building in the 1930s, Patzner and his fellow board members secured a donated land parcel along Meridian Avenue and seized the opportunity for contracting and labor provided by the New Deal–era Public Works Administration, adding in $4,500 from their own tax base to build a new school building. Designed by architect E.J. Breseman and built by contractors Dudley Gunston and Richard Smith, the brick building featured two classrooms, an office and a two-hundred-seat auditorium that was frequently used for community events in the years that followed. The building was completed in 1935, and the students moved into their new schoolhouse midway through the 1935–1936 school year.

Don Glaser recalled going there in grades one through eight. He graduated from eighth grade in 1945. By the late 1940s, Firgrove was becoming more of an elementary school, as both its junior high and high school students were increasingly being sent to Puyallup District locations. As the population on the Hill grew, the local school tax base, relative to that of larger districts, pressured school authorities to eliminate smaller districts. South Hill civic leader Frank Ballou and the Citizens Committee for Education led the charge for consolidation. Consequently, in 1950, the Firgrove and Puyallup School Districts agreed to consolidate. The much larger Puyallup District bordered Firgrove to the north. On March 14 of that year, a proposition calling for the consolidation was submitted to the voters and was approved. Also in 1950, the area around the school was increased by an additional five acres. This provided room for expansion, such as the addition of classrooms and new buildings.

The "modern" 1935 brick Firgrove School replaced the one-room wooden Firgrove School, which had been built in 1895. *Courtesy of South Hill Historical Society.*

Until the 1960s, Firgrove comprised only one building, which was built in the 1930s and still exists as part of the contemporary Firgrove campus, located at 13918 South Meridian Avenue; as of this writing, it is the oldest educational building on the Hill. There were three classrooms and an auditorium. The school offered instruction in grades one through six. Grades one and two were combined in one room, a second area housed classes three and four and grades five and six occupied the third classroom. The auditorium was used by all of the students. Firgrove was not a large school. By October 1959, there were twenty-two children registered in grades one and two, fifteen students were credited to levels three and four and classes five and six had fifteen learners, for a total enrollment of fifty-two students. Attendance numbers varied throughout the school year, as noted in the Parent Teacher Association (PTA) accounts, which used the statistics to award prizes to those rooms that had the best turnout each month.

Mr. Ed Zeiger was the principal at Firgrove during the 1959–1960 school year. He also taught fifth and sixth grade. Over the years, Mr. Zeiger continued his career as an educator, serving as principal at Wildwood Park Elementary School, Pope Elementary School and Sunrise Elementary School (in addition to Stewart Elementary School in the valley) and is now retired and living on South Hill. As a tribute to his distinguished service to the South Hill educational community, a school on Ninety-Fourth Avenue was named in his honor: Zeiger Elementary School.

The records show that the Firgrove community was actively involved in the education of its children. The PTA met monthly and maintained a regular liaison with the school. There was, for example, a room mother assigned to each classroom. Mrs. Mary Glaser was a room mother in 1960. She said it was her job to make sure the students had their birthdays acknowledged and that Christmas festivities, room parties and other special events were organized. These occasions took place in the school auditorium. Specialized clothing for students in certain events was also overseen by the PTA, and money was raised through bake sales and other fundraising drives. The PTA was also concerned with the safety of the children. Members worked closely with the Washington State Patrol to see that selected students were trained in traffic duties. In May 1961, State Patrol sergeant L.H. Thomas presented pins to the school patrol. At one point, the PTA considered clearing paths along Meridian Avenue so that the children could have a safe place to walk while attending school.

## Hazel Whitford Miller Goheen

### By Paul Hackett, March 2005

Meet Hazel Whitford Miller Goheen who was born in Blaine, Washington, on May 3, 1910. When she was a teenager in the late 1920s, times were hard for many people, including the Whitford family, but Hazel was no burden to her family. She was the third daughter. She did not go with a "steady boyfriend" because she was focused on preparing to become a teacher. She went to Bellingham Normal for college. She said:

> *I worked as a grade school janitor two hours Monday through Friday and two and a half hours on Saturday while attending school. Then [I] continued while graduation was going on with the same. I was paid thirty-five cents an hour. This paid my way through normal school. It is too bad boys and girls couldn't pay their way now—it costs so much now.*

In May 1929, nineteen-year-old Hazel did not attend her graduation because she could not afford a formal dress. As she was working after school as a janitor to save up money for appropriate teacher clothes, she opted out of the ceremony. However, on graduation day, no teaching contract came her way.

Her cousin Alvah Huff suggested she send her application to Firgrove School, which she did. She said she would come for a personal interview; they sent the contract immediately, so she signed it and sent it back. Mrs. Winnifred Huff picked her up at the Puyallup Bus Station and took her to meet the school board. When she was introduced to Mrs. Bock, after a bit, Mrs. Bock said, "Are you the teacher?" as she looked down at the five-foot-one-inch petite "girl" before her, dressed in one of the three new dresses she owned. Mrs. Patzner and Mr. Predmore were the two other members of the school board. (Patzner lived just east of the schoolhouse on 136th Street East, and the street was named after him.)

But Hazel was hired, and after that, she got along well with her students. Hazel had good classroom control. She walked to and from the school through the woods. At that time, teachers could not date, smoke or drink and had to be at home by 8:00 p.m.

Hazel Whitford Miller Goheen taught South Hill students in the 1930s and 1940s. *Courtesy of South Hill Historical Society.*

Her pay was one hundred dollars a month plus five dollars for doing the janitorial work in her own room. Of course, pay was by an "interest-bearing warrant." She could cash the warrant "if there was enough tax money on hand." (Some teachers quit because they couldn't afford to teach when they could not cash their warrant.) However, Hazel could always cash the warrants she got. "That was good pay in those days," she said.

She taught twenty-five children in the first through fourth grade. Another teacher taught the fifth through eighth grades. Hazel took the bus to Seattle twice to bring back suitcases of discarded books from the library. She also bought an encyclopedia, which she left at the school. Perle Park was a fourth grader and said he truly found the articles in the encyclopedias Hazel bought interesting. Some of the students came from the Rabbit Farms, where Dorothy (Nelson) lived, as did the Gees. Only about forty students in all lived in the catchment area from $122^{nd}$ to $152^{nd}$ Streets east and west of Meridian Avenue.

In 1929, there were almost no businesses on Meridian Avenue. In the Meridian Avenue and $112^{th}$ Street East area, there were the Miller's Grocery Store and Gas Station and the Willows Dance Hall, where Hazel and her friends Shirley and Enid Wright and Eunice Stover danced to big bands. It cost seventy-five cents for men and twenty-five cents for women to enter the dance hall; Kupfer's home was located on the other corner.

Hazel's tenure at Firgrove School lasted two years until she took up the county superintendent of schools' suggestion that, for her advancement, she should take a teaching job at Woodland School. They offered her $115 and no janitorial work. She taught at Woodland School from 1931 to 1934. When the school bell rang, all of the students would march into the school. (They still do this at Woodland alumni reunions, but they march in place.) Times were hard, so although it cost twenty-five cents a year to be in the Woodland PTA, they made a "local" membership provision to pay only ten cents.

Hazel taught thirty children in the third and fourth grades. "They were really good children," she said. Her students included Robert Litton, Maudine Swalander, Joe Sladek and many "wonderful boys and girls." Bernice Rinehart (whose father was Grange Master) was in the sixth grade and knew Hazel. She "knew both sides," the folks at Woodland school and her friends at the McMillan Grange, including the Patzner, Kehr and Mosolf families. At one meeting, the Woodland people asked Hazel why she went to the McMillan Grange. She told them about the Grange work and what it stood for. They were interested, so she invited the McMillin Grange to come up to Woodland to talk to them. They decided that evening to organize the Fruitland Grange, so named for two "reasons": there was another Woodland Grange in Washington State and the school fronted Fruitland Avenue.

Soon, Hazel was making news in the state Grange work. She was turned down for the drill team due to her height, but she was featured as a princess standing on a bridge in a Grange tableau for the State Grange in Tacoma in 1932.

She was also very active in 4-H work, as was Mrs. Predmore. Hazel led the singing when the county held its countywide meetings several times. Each county went to Pullman in June to participate in statewide activities. One time in the stunt contest, she was "the Spirit of 4-H club work," and Pierce County won the prize (a banner). She had three 4-H clubs at one time because a male club leader could not be found for the boys, so they were a cooking club and had cookouts for supper at Maplewood Springs. She was the county president of 4-H leaders and was later the president of the southwest Washington 4-H leaders. The county had people from Washington, D.C., help communities with interest in 4-H in the 1930s and 1940s; their names were Mr. and Mrs. Jackson, and they came for plays and games. Mr. Knapp and his wife came the next year for plays, acting, lighting and positioning on stage.

In 1934, Hazel taught at Kirby School in the Graham area. The school board wanted her because she had captained a girls' baseball team to two county championships. Her husband-to-be, Clifford Miller, was managing a county gravel crusher, and it was said "there would then be one too many persons working in a family." This problem was solved in 1934, when she married Miller and moved to a home on Stewart Avenue. At that time, Hazel did not teach. In 1938, their only child, Faye, was born. Later, in 1939, Hazel was one of the hundreds of volunteers who built the Fruitland Grange building for $10,000. It is still used today.

In 1942, due to the war effort, many women were employed in the Todd shipyards, and there was a great lack of teachers. Hazel returned to Firgrove School, which, by then, was located on Meridian Avenue. One of her happy moments occurred when she was directing a spoof play, *Henry's Mail-Order Wife*. Her actors included Myra and Bill Geddes, Rufle Breckon, Margaret Felker, Betty and Roy Rinehart and Clifford Miller, her husband. It was such a "laugh-getter success" that many Grange groups asked them to perform it. Again, she taught for three more years.

Later in life, Hazel lived in Canada for twenty years. Later still, she lived in Blaine, the city in which she was born. Her daughter, Faye Miller Serviss, and her husband, Frank, lived in the Puyallup area, so she visited the area quite often.

*Editor's note: Hazel passed away on January 3, 2013, at the age of 102.*

## Puyallup Heights School

The Forest Grove School District (the school's name was later changed to the Puyallup Heights School) has been gone since 1944. However, the old schoolhouse remained a center of community activity long after that date. From its beginnings, the school and its adjoining community center served as a center of social life for over sixty years. The school district was established in 1910, after South Hill's other districts, Woodland and Firgrove, had already been established. By 1910, there were enough school-age children living on the crest of the Hill and just south of it to justify them having their own school.

*Above*: The Puyallup Heights School (1911–1944). Today, the Meridian Firs Apartments and a 7-Eleven occupy this site at the corner of Thirty-First Avenue Southeast and Meridian. *Courtesy of South Hill Historical Society.*

*Left*: John and Edith Mosolf. *Courtesy of Ruth Anderson.*

An early written record describing the creation of Forest Grove School District is a paper that was written by Edith Mosolf in 1936. Her husband, John Mosolf, was a part of a group of neighbors who petitioned for the school's creation.

## School District No. 114

### *By Edith Peters Mosolf, 1936*

For many years, the population of what is now School District No. 114 remained unchanged. The earliest settlers were the Kupfers and Mosolfs: Mr. Alois Kupfer, with his family settling here in 1879, and George Mosolf, a senior in 1890. Their children attended the Woodland School. In 1900, A.H. Miller moved his family from Puyallup into this district, and the William Price family came a few years later. The children from these families went to the Puyallup schools.

By 1910, however, a great many changes had taken place. Several families—the Zimmermans, Goelzers and Enslins—had moved here from the east and had several children of school age. The matter of organizing a new school district was generally discussed, but nothing special had been done about it until one Sunday evening, when we had as guests my father, A.N. Miller, Louis Kupfer and his sister, Lizzie. The conversation was about the many new families in our community and the need of a petition to create a school closer than Puyallup.

This petition was later presented to the county school superintendent, and in the spring of 1910, a meeting was attended by C.C. Hale, Louis Kupfer and Charles Fullager, representing the Fir Grove District from which we hoped to grab a few sections, and Miles Edgerton and John Mosolf. After some discussion, our petition was granted, and we were given Sections No. 2, 3, 10, 11, one half of Section No. 4 and one half of Section No. 9. It was not a very large district, but it was quite valuable because, at that time, it contained much timber land.

In 1911, our present school was built at an approximate cost of $1,800. The contract was awarded to S.C. Nicholson. Warrants were issued to pay for our building and were retired, I believe, in about one year. Our taxes, of course, were much higher for a time, and a few nonresident property owners registered a kick, but we of the district thought the money well spent.

At the present time, I wish to pay a tribute to our only bachelor director, Mr. Louis Kupfer, who, in those early days, gave so generously of his time and business ability in administering the affairs of the district. Many admired the location of our school and the beautiful grove of fir trees surrounding it. That the trees were left standing was due to the suggestion of another faithful director, the late Mr. William Goelzer.

In September 1911, our new building was ready, with Miss Dorsey installed as the first teacher. A neat sign inscribed, "Forest Grove School," the work of Herbert Taylor, Allen and Roy Goelzer, hung over the front steps. Due to the similarity of the names—Forest Grove and Fir Grove—we later changed this name to Puyallup Heights.

The school now became the center of the social life of the community. Entertainments were held here and, as is the custom in rural communities, Sunday school and church also. A library was started, with Mr. William Goelzer and Miss Lizzie Kupfer being appointed to select the books. No doubt, some of those old volumes are still in existence. On January 1, 1915, the Puyallup Heights Improvement Club was organized and held monthly meetings at the schoolhouse for many years. This club took an active interest in school affairs, sponsoring many projects of value. The recreation hall was built in the summer of 1915. Later, a kitchen was added to this building by the Improvement Club. This club also assisted materially in the purchase of a piano for the school and in installing a lighting plant.

Personally, I am very proud of our little school—proud that my four children passed the eight grades here well-equipped to enter high school in town.

And I am also sure we who helped to establish this district are proud of the boys and girls who were the first pupils here, many of whom, now grown to manhood and womanhood, have established homes of culture and refinement in our midst. Happy, too, to think that much good was accomplished by those who had the vision twenty-seven years ago to organize and establish School District No. 114.

## Getting to High School

Settlers formed elementary schools early, but they did not form high schools. Rogers High School was not opened until 1968. Before Rogers, students had to make their way to high schools elsewhere. The most common destination was Puyallup High School.

Getting to Puyallup High School from the Hill was not easy, but generations of students made the effort. Before World War II, there was no locally organized educational transportation system, and Puyallup graduates from the Hill would later tell stories about their walking routes to the high school. Horse and buggies were sometimes used, and other accounts tell of hitching rides in various ways.

Around the time of World War II, an organized bus system was started. Many old timers remember the first bus as "that old double-decker." It was a vehicle previously used by—or perhaps leased from—the Blue-Gray Lines, a well-known local company. It was a Pickwick, painted blue and gray, with two decks and seats for about thirty students. The stairway to the second level was located inside. It was said that you could sit in the upper deck and look down into the lower half through the cracks in the floor. It was used until June 1950, when it was replaced by a single-deck vehicle. The reason for the change was probably the damage that resulted when students overturned the double-decker.

The bus route came from Puyallup, went up the hill and then headed south on Meridian Avenue; it went back the same way. During snowstorms, the bus didn't run, as it couldn't get up the hill. Student pickups were made at various places, but initially, the bus didn't travel off Meridian Avenue. Moreover, it did not go very far south. Bob Ballou remembers it turning around at 152$^{nd}$ Street. Mary Glaser recalled that, around 1959, the route went as far as Thun Field. It all depended on the number of students who needed transport. Later, there were some side routes, especially through Rabbit Farms.

Students had to get from their homes to the bus route on their own. Most walked. Joan Parks Vosler and her sisters walked from around present-day Rogers High School to Meridian Avenue, a distance of roughly three-quarters of a mile. They waited for the bus in Lyman's gas station. Bob Ballou lived on Meridian Avenue but walked to Firgrove School for pickup. Don Glaser recalled walking about a mile and a quarter. Katie Gabrielson Bennett walked from 86$^{th}$ Street, just over one mile.

# 5
# MERIDIAN AVENUE AND OTHER ROADS

Meridian Avenue is the traffic artery that runs through South Hill. It is also the community's oldest planned road, dating from the late 1800s. The route was created by local citizens and the Pierce County government working together.

As noted previously, the Donation Land Claim Act of 1850 authorized the land surveys throughout the Pacific Northwest. First, a grid system was established. To begin, a point was chosen near the intersection of the Columbia and Willamette Rivers in what is now the city of Portland, Oregon. Then, by astronomical observations, an imaginary north–south line was created through that point and named the "Willamette Meridian." Next, an imagined east–west line was fabricated. It was given the name "Range." So, it was from this intersection, along the Meridian and Range lines, that the Pacific Northwest was surveyed.

Today, a north–south line through the center of South Hill, designated in the 1800s as Township 19, lies on a meridian line that is parallel to the referenced Willamette Meridian and is four townships east of it. On South Hill, this line is named Meridian Avenue.

On December 29, 1888, the Pierce County commissioners received a petition to "lay out" and "establish" a new thoroughfare on South Hill. The road was to begin at the Puyallup "town" line and proceed south for approximately five miles, ending at the corner of a farm owned by Carl "Swamp" Muehler. Eighty-seven citizens signed the request, and it was accepted by the commissioners on February 4, 1889. A bond in the amount of $200 was required to pay for the survey, and it was furnished by Harvey

## A Community History

M. Ball and George Wood. When the road was completed, it was named in their honor.

The survey for the road was done over five days, starting on April 30, 1889. J.C. Kincaid and William Shuman were appointed as the "viewers." They hired three assistants: John Spencer, Veriin Raymoure and C.D. Bailets. During that period, land distances were measured by dragging an iron chain over the route. C.S. Bailets was employed as a chainman. The chain comprised one hundred links and was sixty-six feet long. Also, it was customary to mark established survey points by cutting notches or symbols onto trees. To do this—and to clear the way where necessary—two axemen were engaged: George Mercy and F.M. Atinnette. So, the survey party consisted of eight people.

In this September 1971 photograph that was ordered by Allstate Insurance Company, construction was underway for the completion of State Route 512, and Meridian Avenue was temporarily rerouted over excavated dirt from the highway project, with a reduced speed limit of 25 miles per hour. The project resulted in a revised T intersection on Meridian Avenue at the top of the hill, connecting Meridian Avenue and 104th Street East (today's 31st Avenue Southwest). Real estate signs at 110th Street East (today's 37th Avenue East) advertised the new Parkwood and Forest Green developments. *Courtesy of Tacoma Public Library, Richards Studio Collection, D1608144.*

The surveyors started at the Puyallup town line, around the point where today's Meridian and Pioneer Avenues intersect. The first couple of miles were over cleared land and on a gently rising slope. At most points, there were no trees nearby to make marks, so stakes were used to identify distances. By mile three, they had gone through thick groves of timber. This would have been at the top of the Hill, around present day 39th Street (112th). Working south, through miles three and four, they saw large trees and considerable swampy land. Distances then were recorded by marking trees, both fir and cottonwood, which were noted as being up to twenty-four inches in diameter. Mile four ended at today's 144th Street. Around present-day 160th Street, the survey team turned east and ended its work at the corner of today's 110th Avenue; this was roughly five miles from the starting point. The land became less swampy as the surveyors approached the farm

The bill for surveying the road was $102.30. Kincaid, Sherman and Raymoure each received $10.00 for five days of labor. Spencer and Stinette were paid $12.00. George Mercy was paid $12.00 and Bailets $2.00. Other charges on the May 7, 1889 invoice were for writing and platting the results and for mileage.

When the road was built, it was thirty feet wide and constructed with regular county labor. There is no indication that a contractor was involved. It was little more than a wide, muddy path. Gradually, it was extended. The surface was improved from time to time, first with gravel and later with asphalt. In January 1905, forty-three residents wrote to the county commission, asking for "straightening, grading and graveling of one mile of Ball & Wood Road." Early pavement was only on the east side to provide a smooth surface for transporting farm produce to market. The road served the public satisfactorily as a farm-to-market path until well after World War II.

In both 1910 and 1913, petitions from local people got the road extended southward, eventually to Graham. The additions were not on the modern line of Meridian Avenue, however, but were south, on present day 110th Avenue, and across what is now the closed county landfill. When it was completed, the road from 160th Street southward was named the "Puyallup–Graham Road." Official maps as late as the 1960s show both names on the continuous road. It was not until the 1920s that Meridian Avenue was rerouted to its present location.

By the late 1920s, it was clear that the entire road needed to be paved. Of particular concern was the ten-mile section ending at Graham. A grassroots citizen effort was undertaken to improve the road. This effort eventually proved successful, and the completion of the project was considered so important that it was a cause for celebration.

# A Community History

Some five hundred people came to a dedication ceremony on Friday, August 14, 1931, at the Willows, the popular South Hill dance hall and meeting place located near the present-day intersection of Meridian Avenue and 39th Street. The commemoration was sponsored and structured by three organizations: the Puyallup Heights Improvement Club, the Puyallup Chamber of Commerce and the Puyallup Kiwanis Club. They called it an "Inter-Community Celebration." The affair was not a cut-the-ribbon-and-go-home event. The ceremony started with a community singing session, followed by speeches from a number of prominent people. The orations stressed the importance of the road in bringing communities together and the economic benefit that would then be enjoyed by all. The program also included some solo vocal acts, as well as a comedy skit. Afterward, the group remained for an evening of music and dancing. This was a major event on South Hill. Five hundred people assembling in a rural community for a road dedication was an important and impressive occurrence. At that time, the population of the entire South Hill area was probably no more than a few thousand people.

A second event happened immediately after the party, in the early hours of Saturday, August 15. The festivity did not end until about midnight. About an hour later, the Willows Roadhouse burned to the ground. Arson was suspected, as locks had been broken, and the odor of gasoline was evident. The fire did not appear to have any connection with the commemoration that had just been held.

A once-common identifier that never made it into the official records—but one that was used regularly by local folks—was "Farm to Market Road." During the Hill's agricultural period, there was always a problem of how to get crops to markets. In the early days, the highway was a gravel road, and some local crops were delicate, like berries. They were often damaged when transported. So, in 1936, the county paved a nine-foot-wide strip on the eastern side of the thoroughfare, leaving the west side gravel. The idea was that transports going north to market areas, like Puyallup, would travel on a smooth surface; returning empty, they were to drive on the gravel side. Law enforcement officers often issued citations for driving south on the paved portion.

Over the years, Meridian Avenue has been known by a number of names: Ball-Wood Road, Puyallup-Graham Road, Meridian Street Extension, Farm-to-Market Road and probably others. The simultaneous use of these names, at one point, was a source of confusion, so in the mid-1930s, the name of the entire thoroughfare was changed to reflect its status as a meridian.

South Hill, Washington

## Trolley to South Hill

The Old Line Trolley, TR&P Line (Tacoma Railway & Power Company), Puyallup's first, operated from approximately 1889 to 1919. The trolley line started in Puyallup, then wound its way up the Hill, through Maplewood Springs (south of the Washington State Department of Game, Puyallup Fish Hatchery), to 104th Street East and Woodland Avenue. This was the location of the trolley's Woodland Station for South Hill passengers. From there, it went west through Summit and Midland to Fern Hill and connected with the Tacoma/Spanaway Trolley.

For residents of Puyallup and the Hill, the trolley was, for a time, the only means of public transportation to Tacoma, a very roundabout route for those living in Puyallup. The part of the Old Line between Maplewood Springs and Woodland Station followed a path of least resistance to get from the valley floor to the top of the Hill. This path was the ravine that follows Clarks Creek. The trolley was notorious for its unsound, accident-prone trestle that skirted along the treacherously steep ridge that climbs above the creek and the springs.

The Old Line was eventually replaced by the "Short Line," the Puget Sound Electric Railway, which was a much more direct route from Puyallup to Tacoma. The Short Line Electric Trolley left Puyallup and crossed the Puyallup River, then went west through Firwood and on to a point west of Fife called Willow Junction. From there, it followed what in later years would be Pacific Highway, U.S. 99, which runs into Tacoma's Puyallup Avenue, then moves on to downtown Tacoma.

The era of electric trolleys came to an end in the late 1930s, when buses, which were more versatile and less expensive to operate, rapidly replaced trolleys—not to mention the ever-growing use of private automobiles over roads that were continually being improved.

## Shaw Road

The roads and streets we now use between the Hill and the valley did not exist in the late 1800s. Later on, people walked to Puyallup for supplies using foot paths. One regularly used trail went first to Meeker Junction (the railroad intersection along present-day East Pioneer Avenue), then to Puyallup.

# A Community History

The Old Line Trolley, from Puyallup to Fern Hill, climbs up a steep grade to South Hill. *Courtesy of Wes Perkinson.*

In 1901, a forty-five-year-old carpenter named Chris Shaw, his wife, Mary, and their six children settled in the Puyallup Valley. They had made a long, hard journey from Colorado, through Wyoming, Idaho and Oregon. Shaw, a clever carpenter, modified his large wagon to resemble a modern-day camper, and he built a small buggy that Mary could handle while caring for her baby. Chris Shaw was a Danish immigrant with talent and ingenuity that would benefit any community he was part of. Among his many talents, he was known for his mechanical skills. Before coming to the Puyallup Valley, he attended college to become a minister. His life in Puyallup was spent as a farmer, preacher and carpenter. He became one of the most respected men in Puyallup.

The spot where Shaw built his home, across from where today's Twenty-Fifth Street Southeast and Pioneer Avenue meet, had to be cleared by Shaw and his two eldest sons, Emery and Frank. After four years of clearing his fifteen-acre property and building a house and barn, Shaw had what was called then a "model home and farm." It was featured in the January 7, 1911 *Puyallup Valley Tribune*. The article stated, "The fruit on this place consists of one and one-half acres of Evergreen blackberries, three-

Shaw Road is one of the few roads on the Hill that maintains its historic name. *Courtesy of South Hill Historical Society.*

fourths of an acre of red raspberries and two acres of orchard, principally apples, pears and cherries…ten acres of the farm are in pasturage, and the remainder is devoted to kale, beets and other forage root crops." His crops held production records for kale and beets. Shaw's seventh child was born in 1904, giving him and his wife three sons and four daughters. Lightning killed their eldest son, Emery, when he was twenty-five, in 1912. The Shaw farm was considered an "oasis." The Shaws would take in homeless people. After a good meal, Chris Shaw, the preacher, would try to convert them, telling them of the gospel.

In 1916, what is now Shaw Road was a mere trail along which some families lived. Wild animals often stalked those who traveled this path. According to maps in the county files, the original path was built on an "Old Tramway Grade," which had probably been used to move logs from cuttings on the Hill to various sawmills in Puyallup in earlier times. Since Shaw's son Frank and Guy Clifford then owned property along the route, they felt compelled to convert the existing path into a road. Building the road became a Shaw family project. Frank Shaw was a born engineer; he and Guy Clifford combined their efforts (Clifford later married Frank Shaw's sister, Laura).

Like most roads on South Hill, Shaw Road was not completed as part of one big construction job. Rather, it was developed in phases—or as small sections—one after the other, over a period of time. It now appears that the first section, about a mile in length, had its roots in 1914. Sometime that year, petitions to establish Shaw Road were submitted to the Pierce County commissioners. County records include two different petitions, and both are undated. Sixteen property owners signed one petition, which appears to have been the initial request to establish the road. It carries the appeal that "said road be known as the Shaw County Road." One member of the Shaw family is among the signers: Mrs. C.B. Shaw. Eleven property owners, including Chris Shaw, signed the other application, which suggested that the road should be one mile in length. As a result of these requests, the county engineer undertook a survey of the proposed road and filed a report dated December 15, 1914. The engineer also filed a document titled "Field Notes," which show that his survey was undertaken between October 3 and 21, 1914.

After considering the requests made by citizens and approving the work done by the county engineer, Pierce County commissioners, on November 5, 1915, approved a road that was 3,943 feet (three-quarters of a mile) long, crossing Section 35 of Township 20. The commissioners also approved the name "Shaw County Road" at that time. The road was completed in 1920. The state road commissioner at the time was highly impressed, calling it remarkable. The commissioner insisted that it be named Shaw Road, as it was the Shaw family and spouses who donated the equipment, time and money to make it possible.

The original road did not run in a straight north–south line to Pioneer Avenue as it does now. At the bottom of South Hill, the original constructors routed it westward on what is now Twelfth Avenue Southeast. The road was then built along the bottom edge of the Hill until it reached a point that is now Twenty-Fifth Street Southeast. Here, it was again directed north and was terminated at Pioneer Avenue, across from the Shaw family farmhouse. The road was not straightened to its current configuration until 1941.

## Glaser Road

At one time on South Hill, there were innumerable road names in use. Unfortunately, there was no particular order in this accumulation, as they had evolved as the county developed. County officials often awarded route names as a way to honor people who lived in the area or to recognize families who had been active in getting particular roads built (for example, Collins Road, Shaw Road, Ball-Wood Road and others).

Glaser Road is an example of a thoroughfare that was named for a specific family. It was probably one of the shortest highways in the county (about one-half mile in length) and was situated in a north–south direction

## Neighbor Frank Shaw

### By Jerry Bates

Not long after Pete and Linda Ziemke moved into their new home and nursery off Shaw Road in the 1970s, an elderly neighbor, bent with age, came walking up the driveway, knocked on the door and introduced himself. His name was Frank Shaw. Many similar visits would follow. Pete said he was "shrewd," careful to visit when he saw Linda's car at the house. "He loved Linda's coffee—and we loved the old man and talking to him." Pete enjoyed listening to Frank's stories and would "pick his brain."

Frank once owned all the land along Shaw road, including Pete's property. Shaw Road's "nasty curves," as Frank explained, were due to "the county screwing up my original survey." When Old Frank learned Pete used to sing in gospel quartets and his brother was a preacher, Frank loudly announced, "I used to know Aimee Semple McPherson!" (She was an evangelist and media celebrity of the 1920s and 1930s.) He wanted to attend Pete's brother's church. "We took him to church and to the choir loft and sang—he loved it!" said Pete.

Frank Shaw, seen here in his nineties. *Courtesy of Ruth Anderson.*

# A Community History

> Frank invited Pete to his home. "He was very eclectic and crafty," said Pete. For example, a salvaged grand piano from a Puyallup High School fire, with its legs burned off, was mounted on the wall—it had been made into a China cabinet. Out in his barn, he had the horse-drawn wagon that was used by his father to travel west—its current status is unknown.
>
> Frank told many stories, including one about Ezra Meeker. While bouncing up the Hill in his new Model T Ford, Meeker spooked Frank's draft horses, Maude and Millie, who were hard at work, pulling a huge log. Infuriated, Frank confronted Meeker. The young man slugged him under the chin, reportedly putting the historic pioneer on his back. Pete continued, "Frank could quote scripture almost as good as my Pentecostal preaching brother! Afterwards, he would grin and follow with a little 'smut' joke."
>
> One day, an ambulance was in front of Frank's house. Pete ran over—Frank had passed away. Pete ran inside, and there was Frank, lying in his bed, fully dressed in his "Sunday-go-to-meeting" suit. The bed he was conceived in was the same bed in which he died.

on what is now 122nd Avenue East. It was created in 1926, when Nicholas Glaser and his wife, Barbara, donated frontage on the east side of their farm for its construction.

The Glaser family's roots go back to Germany, but Nicholas Glaser was born in Wilkes Barre, Pennsylvania, in 1859. He grew up in that state, and during his early years, he made his living in real estate. He was in his fifties when he migrated to the Northwest. Nicholas apparently acquired considerable land throughout the South Sound area, but in particular, in 1912, he bought and settled on three forty-acre tracts on South Hill, located just southwest of the Tacoma Water Reservoir. The present-day location of these lots would be on the west and north side of the intersection of 122nd Avenue and 144th Street.

Between 1912 and 1926, neither 122nd Avenue nor 144th Street existed. People who lived in that part of South Hill had no road system other than some unofficial primitive wagon trails that gave them access to the 1853 Military Road (Naches Trail). But in the early 1900s, a passage called Reservoir Road (now 136th Street) was built to service the Tacoma Water

The location of the Nicholas Glaser farm. *Courtesy of Jerry Bates and the South Hill Historical Society.*

Wayne and Don Glaser holding historic road signs before they were mounted at intersections in 2008. *Courtesy of Don and Mary Glaser.*

Reservoir. This path proved useful to local people and provided passageways to both the Ball-Wood Road (now Meridian Avenue) and old Military Road. Over the years, the Glasers also used these roads and did so by first traveling on a trail by the east side of their farm.

Ultimately, to legalize the unauthorized wagon trail on the east side of the farm and to more formally open up the farm to outside areas, the Glaser family donated a strip of land that was thirty feet wide for a lawful road. On May 20, 1926, the county accepted the gift and subsequently named the road in honor of the family.

## Mitchell-Gould Road

A historic road sign posted at the corner of Meridian Avenue and 152nd Street declares that 152nd Street was at one time known as Mitchell-Gould Road. This road was developed in two phases.

It all started on December 2, 1925, when the county commission approved a proposal, based on a survey done by the county engineer in April 1925, to build a road across the east–west center of Section 21 of Township 19. The technical specifications describing where it would be built depicts the location of present day 152nd Street. The road, as it was originally built, started at Meridian Avenue and went in a westerly direction. It did not cross Meridian Avenue to the east, but it ended at the western boundary of Section 21, or, to quote the County Order, "the total length being 1 mile and 115.0 feet." The development of the road was justified, as "there [was] no other road which [was] of equal utility for the citizens residing in the vicinity of said proposed road, the terminal points, general course and length."

Why was it called Mitchell-Gould Road? Mr. J.B. Mitchell owned the property at what is now the northwest corner of Meridian Avenue and 152nd Street, and he donated land. The Gould family owned a farm at the western terminus. While they did not donate land, their dairy operation was probably the real reason it was built. It provided an outlet for their products. Thus, the road was named for the two landowners at each end of the project.

The second phase of development occurred in 1931. In June of that year, the county received a petition from twenty-two citizens who lived in the area, requesting that Mitchell-Gould Road be extended to the west to connect with what is now Canyon Road (then known as Malcolm McLarty Road). The county engineer surveyed a route, and various landowners donated land. The project was approved. Rather than give the new road a second name, it was called the Mitchell-Gould Extension, and it is so recorded in the county archives.

The extension did not follow the same westerly direction as the original road because of the problem of crossing Cedar Swamp. So, the road was extended in a westerly direction to a point where it intersects present-day 78th Avenue. Then, construction headed south, to today's 156th Street (about one-half mile). The development then was moved westerly, to today's 74th Avenue (about one-quarter mile). On 74th Avenue, the road was advanced south, to the intersection of modern-day 160th Street. Finally, it was built along that path to what is now Canyon Road. All this zigzagging was done to get around Cedar Swamp.

When laying out the extension, it was discovered that a farmhouse, the homestead of the Wilber F. Gould family, was located on the section line, just east of the intersection. The Goulds had acquired the 160-acre farm in 1889. While it had been modified several times, the original building was still in place, and the road path, as envisioned, would require constructing it directly through the house. Going around it solved the problem.

By 1931, the Gould family no longer lived in the original house. In 1912, they had built a new home farther east on the property. The old house was still being used, however, as a home for Wilber's son and wife. The original house is no longer there. It remained on the property until about 1951, when the Blyton family, who, by then, owned the old Gould property, took it down. In fact, all the original structures in that area have been removed for a modern subdivision. All that is left is the divergence in an otherwise straight roadway.

So, while Mitchell-Gould Road started out as being the equivalent of today's 152nd Street, it eventually evolved into a rather complicated road system.

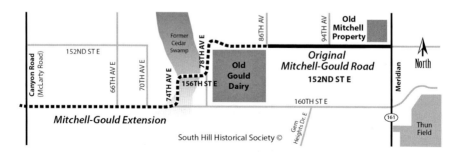

Historic Mitchell-Gould Road, today's 152nd Street. *Courtesy of Jerry Bates and the South Hill Historical Society.*

# A Community History

## Growing Up on Mitchell-Gould Road

In the early 1940s, young Gloria George moved with her family onto the Hill; they had bought and settled on a forty-acre plot fronting on what is now 152$^{nd}$ Street (then known as Mitchell-Gould Road), at its juncture with 94$^{th}$ Avenue. Gloria explained that her family's house and property was on the south side of Mitchell-Gould Road and was six-tenths of a mile west of Meridian Avenue. The land had been bought from Mr. J.H. Turnmire. Earlier, the land had been part of the Weyerhaeuser Timber Company's holdings.

Gloria remembered that, when she was young, her family lived in a typical farmhouse; it had an open garage and a fairly good-sized barn. When her parents initially bought the property, they also inherited "Grandma," a jersey cow, in the deal. During World War II, Mrs. George sold milk and butter that she made from the milk produced by that cow. Also, during the early days, the family kept two riding horses. Gloria's recollection from her childhood was that the road now known as Ninety-Fourth Avenue was really nothing more than a dirt "path." The local people didn't use it often. This was because very few families lived on it, and additionally, the roadbed was almost always in extremely bad shape—consisting primarily of mud, ruts and muddy potholes.

Interestingly, Gloria recollected major water problems during her family's early days on their farm. The problem wasn't that there was too much water; rather, there was not enough. She recalled that when her father bought the farm, there was a water well on the property that was about thirty feet deep. The family was not accustomed to conservation, however, as they had been urban dwellers before moving to the Hill, so they proceeded to draw down the reservoir faster than it could be replenished by nature. As a consequence, they eventually had to haul water from a source located at the intersection of Collins Road (now 128$^{th}$ Street) and Meridian Avenue. That site was a country store that was owned by Mr. Lyman, and it was located alongside the Tacoma City water line, which ran from its reservoir on South Hill to the city of Tacoma. Gloria recollected that her father, Mr. George, would go to the store, fill two fifty-gallon barrel, and then haul them home for the family to use. This transported liquid was also the only source of water for the family's animals.

There were few families living in this vicinity in the 1940s, so when going to school, the local children all walked to Meridian Avenue to catch the buses to Firgrove School. Gloria recalled that, when going to school during

World War II, she rode in a double-decker bus that was operated by the Blue-Gray Line. However, that transportation practice was altered after the war years. The students still continued to ride buses that were operated by a private company for a while, but the procedure was changed when the Puyallup School District was consolidated with a number of other smaller local districts. Gloria graduated from Puyallup High School in 1947.

Gloria recalled some of the recreational activities that young people tried during the winter. For example, she recounted specifically one of the things they did when it got cold enough for the local water ponds to freeze. When these conditions were discovered, the local kids got together and went to the Massey Pond, where they played games on the ice. The Massey Pond was a well-known water hole near the present-day corner of 110$^{th}$ Avenue and 152$^{nd}$ Street. When it was frozen, those who had sleds would take them on the ice. The boys would pull the sleds as fast as they could, swing them around and around and then let them go. It was a kind of "crack the whip" sport that was played on ice. "What a great time we all had!" said Gloria.

When Gloria married Chris O'Kelly, a 1942 graduate of Eatonville High School, her family gave them ten acres of land from the original forty acres they owned. It was located on the eastern end of the original farm. This parcel contains a mine, which Chris noted was a source of gravel used for one of the many upgrades of Meridian Avenue. Chris and Gloria built their own house on this land and moved into it in December 1954; they lived there for the remainder of their years together. Gloria's family continued to live on the original farm until the late 1960s, when Gloria's mother sold the other thirty acres.

The O'Kellys believed that the only prominent business activity in the Mitchell-Gould corridor during the 1940s was a dairy that was located at its western end. It was known as the Gould Dairy and prospered for many years. That dairy land was later known as the Blyton Farm, and it is now a major housing project.

## The Woodland Bus Company

During the early development of the Hill, a community transportation infrastructure did not exist. During the logging period and the small farm era, residents were responsible for their own transport. There was, however, always a need for conveyance for those who did not have private means. For about a forty-year period, that necessity was satisfied by the Woodland Bus Company. The Woodland Bus Company was established in 1934 by W.H. Herbert and Russell E. Smith. It connected the Willows on South Hill (Thirty-Ninth Street and Meridian Avenue) with Tacoma via the communities of Midland, Collins, Summit View and Woodland.

A labor dispute has been credited as the reason for forming the company. In 1934, the franchise for operating buses to South Hill was held by the Tacoma Bus Company. Drivers of that period were paid about four dollars a day. Russell Smith was one such operator. Thinking the pay was inadequate, the workers went on strike, demanding six dollars a day. The bus company refused and filed for abandonment of the franchise. The displaced drivers then got together and divided up the old route structure. Focusing on the Tacoma–South Hill segment, Herbert and Smith (who were brothers-in-law) secured approval from the Washington State Department of Public Works to create a bus route, doing business as the Woodland Bus Company. Herbert's son Cecil later wrote an account of the Woodland Bus Company's history:

> *In November of 1934, Mom and Dad moved from Gig Harbor to a house on Woodland Road. On December the 11, 1934, the new bus company started operations with a 1923 White 33-passenger bus, purchased from the Longview Public Service Co. for $900.00.*
>
> *The communities served were Tacoma to Midland–Collins–Summit View–Woodland–the Willows. The company was totally operated by Dad and Uncle Russell—Uncle Russell as main driver, and Dad as a driver and mechanic. An old three-stall garage, located next to the Woodland Grocery, was leased for $1.00 per year. Business was slow getting started but picked up fairly rapidly.*

During the 1930s, the company enjoyed steady but modest business success. At first, only one bus was used, but others were added as resources permitted. This business model changed in the early 1940s. World War II was starting, gas rationing was put into effect, civilian driving was curbed, and jobs opened up in the defense industries around Tacoma. This all combined to increase bus ridership throughout the war years. The company prospered.

After World War II, business remained good, but it was no longer growing. Russell Smith sold his share in the company to W.H. Herbert's son Cecil, Smith's nephew, in 1949. In 1952, they sold the company to Stan Ratcliff. He also owned the Waller Road-Summit Bus Company. He subsequently merged the two and continued to operate the routes using the Woodland Bus Company as the name. He managed the enterprise for a number of years. It changed hands a couple of times in the 1960s and 1970s. In 1979, the firm was integrated into the newly created Pierce Transit system, which still holds the franchise today.

# 6
# RURAL LIFE

Don Glaser once encountered what he called the "ghost horse of South Hill." It was during the summer months of the late 1940s. Don and a group of his friends were exploring the backcountry of South Hill—an area we now call the Sunrise Community, near Emerald Ridge High School. It was late in the day and almost dark. They had no lights on their 1917 Model T truck. As they made their way down a dark road, they suddenly saw a herd of horses running alongside of them. One of the horses was white. It shimmered like a ghost in the poor light. Ever since, Don Glaser has called it the ghost horse of South Hill.

Herds of horses once roamed about South Hill. Bears were also common. Elk and deer were seen regularly. And there were the farms with their domesticated animals. The Glaser family has lived on South Hill, near the Tacoma water reservoir, since the early 1900s. Several generations have grown up on the Hill, and many still call it home. Those who travel Shaw Road and 122$^{nd}$ Avenue may notice a historical road marker called Glaser Road, which commemorates the family's presence in the area.

Wayne and Don Glaser were born on the Hill. Both lived near their birthplace as adults. They reported that, in the 1930s, the Hill was essentially brushland. There was, however, considerable amounts of second-generation timber. Few roads existed, and those that did were primitive. Reportedly, one could safely shoot a rifle in any direction. It was not uncommon to see bears roaming around, and residents would scare them by firing shotguns.

Before World War II, there was no utility infrastructure on the Hill. The Glaser boys reported that, when they were growing up, there was no electricity and no telephone and their water came from a well near their house. Water had to be carried by hand. There were no indoor toilets; pit toilets were used, and the Glasers had a three-hole pit for the entire family.

Like other rural boys, the Glaser children had chores to do each day. They milked cows in the evenings; hogs were fed or slopped; and they gathered eggs in the hen house. They took turns turning a machine called a separator, which divided milk and cream. And, of course, they did school homework. The Glaser youngsters attended Firgrove School, over the years, going to both the old and the new one. They walked about a mile and a half to get there. The boys insisted that school was a pleasure. In addition to the learning process, Don remembered playing marbles, flying kites and going over the fence to play in the brush. He noted that parents came to the school and cooked lunches. Ice skating on the many ponds around South Hill was a favorite recreational pastime. Unfortunately, most of the ponds have now been filled in or drained.

At the time, members of the Glaser clan did not consider themselves farmers. They were loggers. The Saint Paul Tacoma Lumber Company was a big employer at the time; many local people eitherworked for that company or a competitor.

## Christmas on the Hill

During the Christmas season, people usually cut Christmas trees on their own farms or from a neighbor's. Decorations for their homes and trees were usually homemade. Ornaments were shaped from paper and strung across windows and around trees. Since few had electricity, there were no brightly lighted displays.

Local shopping was usually done at Willows Corner. An occasional trip to Puyallup or Tacoma might have been made, but they were not made very often. Special gifts for children were ordered from mail-order catalogs like *Sears & Roebuck*. Homemade clothes were common gifts for children. Mary Glaser remembered making a variety of clothes for her family. Don Glaser was good at woodworking, and over the years, he made many Christmas toys, like small dump trucks, steam shovels and "tommy guns" for boys and baby carriages for girls.

Firgrove School usually sponsored a Christmas play that most children participated in, but other community-wide holiday events were uncommon.

## The Hilderbrand Home on the Hill

*By Joan Parks Vosler*

William Hilderbrand was one of the original settlers on South Hill. He arrived in Washington State in 1890 with his brother Jim. Soon after that, he sent for his mother, Eliza, and sisters, Minetta, Phoebe and Myra, who arrived by train from Mount Pleasant, Iowa.

Bill's property was located on historic James B. Collins Road (now 128th Street East) and the Naches Trail, a spur of the Tacoma Eastern Railroad that cut through the southeast corner of his property. This same Tacoma Eastern Railroad constructed the National Park Inn at Longmire in 1906. The Edison Electric Logging Company had a spur connecting to the Tacoma Eastern Railroad to facilitate the logging operations during the 1920s. This area was heavily logged at the time, and after logging operations stopped, the area was known as the stump farms, later the Half Dollar Berry Tracts. Bill's personal property of two and a half acres joined the property of his sister Myra and her husband, Robert Steele. The five acres behind their property belonged to Uncle Bill. The twenty acres behind their property was purchased by Bill and later sold to the Steeles. The next parcel of land comprised five acres, and Bill purchased this property in 1920 for his mother, Eliza Ellen Hilderbrand. He built her a home, and she lived there until she fell and broke her hip. She was cared for by her daughter Myra until her death. Her grandson Weldon Parks was killed while loading a flat car; it came uncoupled and crushed him. He was fifteen at the time.

Bill Hilderbrand owned a donkey engine and pulled the loaded cars up the hill after they were loaded in the large gulch that circled down and around the logging area. He used the donkey engine to pull logs up for our log home, which was situated next to Great-Grandma's on the next five-acre plat. In front of our property, the Old Military Road (Naches Trail) crossed and continued down the hill across Ninth Street (now Ninety-Fourth Avenue East) and continued at an adjacent angle toward the Old Mill Dance Hall. When I was young, it

> was known as the Klondike. Neighbors met there on Saturday nights to dance. The music was provided by residents who brought their instruments. The fireplaces were fired up by my uncle Stan Washburn, the brother to my mother, Olive Parks. Refreshments were provided by the women.
>
> South Hill was not very populated when we were growing up. Our world revolved around Great-Uncle William Hilderbrand and his sister Myra Hilderbrand Steele. So, you can see we were surrounded by relatives. Until our log home was built in 1941, we lived on the twenty acres. This is where I lived until I was ten years old, so my childhood was confined to this property. Was it boring? No way. We had all these acres to roam and play on.

## Oil and Gas on South Hill?

In 1937, some two thousand acres of South Hill land were designated as an area for oil and gas exploration. In the legal papers for this proposed undertaking, a physical district on the Hill was outlined and named for purposes of exploration; it was called Community Number One. Community Number One was positioned mostly—but not entirely—on the east side of Meridian Avenue. The northern boundary was 128th Street, between Meridian and 122nd Avenues. The east side was bounded by 122nd Avenue, which ran north–south between 128th and 160th Streets. On the west side, most of the border was north–south Meridian Avenue, except for a small fraction on the west side between 144th and 152nd Streets. In this region, the western edge was 88th Avenue. The southern periphery was east–west 152nd Street between 88th and 110th Avenues, and then it ran along 160th Street to 122nd Avenue.

Community Number One was the core of what is now South Hill. It encompassed the present-day commercial districts along the east side of Meridian Avenue, between 128th and 160th Streets. It also comprised all of the present-day housing areas located between Meridian and 122nd Avenues, south to the Sunrise Shopping Center. The area where Pope Elementary School is located was also part of the plan.

The agreement was to be in force for twenty years. There were some exceptions to that limit but only if there were operating wells at the end of the period. For purposes of exploration, the entire designated area was considered one property, even though there were many owners of acreage within its boundaries. As compensation, the various land title holders were to share pro rata in all returns and royalties in proportion to the number of acres they owned in relation to the number of acres covered by the entire community.

So what happened to the oil? When examining the designated district now, for example, it will be observed that no oil pumping rigs are visible; as a matter of fact, there is no evidence that they ever existed. No physical confirmation of oil derricks for drilling can be found. While it is a fact that Community Number One was legally established, there are no additional records showing that any exploration ever took place within its boundaries. Thus, it appears that the community went out of existence in 1957 as planned.

# The 1939 Directory

South Hill was initially a timber-producing area. It then evolved into a community of large farms. This was followed by a period when small farms were the run-of-the-mill. These small holdings were gradually subdivided into more dense developments in the form of housing tracts. Unfortunately, there are few benchmarks that can be used to precisely measure the transitions through these stages. But one point of reference does exist: a 1939 directory of the Puyallup Valley. Included in this study are inputs from the city of Puyallup, as well as listings from the three rural postal routes that originated at the downtown post office. South Hill (called Puyallup Heights) was included, since Postal Route Number Two covered most the Hill.

From the post office, Route Two, during the mid- to late 1930s, went east along Pioneer Avenue to that route's junction with the Orting Highway. It then traveled south to the community of McMillin. At that point, after some local coverage, the track turned west and moved on to South Hill. It then generally zigzagged around what is now Meridian Avenue in a northerly direction back to downtown Puyallup. In this compilation, the names of the people who lived along the postal routes are identified, as well as their postal box numbers, occupations and, in most cases, street addresses.

This study, which was made just before World War II, illustrates one era for South Hill. Farming occupations, for example, were a big deal, with about one-third (32 percent) of the residents classifying themselves as farmers. Listed in the summary were such activities as general farming, ranching, growing bulbs, rabbit farming, berry growing and other such doings. But while many kinds of agricultural efforts were declared by residents, they did not constitute the largest occupational group. The largest set listed themselves as unskilled laboring individuals; 41 percent classified themselves in this way. Together, farming and unskilled laborers accounted for almost three-quarters (73 percent) of the people on the Hill. During this same period, skilled workers made up 14 percent of the occupations listed. Included were electricians, lineman, loggers, mechanics, painters and other similar pursuits. Professional workers accounted for only 3 percent of the total population; included in this listing were schoolteachers, nurses, surveyors, preachers and the like. There were no physicians or lawyers registered. Of the remaining 10 percent, about half were retired people. The other 5 percent claimed to be proprietors of various businesses—for example, the owner of the Willows Tavern.

## Lieutenant Leonard Humiston

South Hill produced some notable heroes during World War II. It is worth mentioning one, Leonard Humiston, who grew up near the location where Bethany Baptist Church now stands. He attended the Puyallup Heights School and graduated from Puyallup High School in 1935. He joined the army air corps right out of school, and by December 6, 1941, he was dispatched to the Philippines from an airfield in California. The formation of airplanes bound for the Philippines had to stop for refueling at Hickam Air Base in Hawaii. As they approached on the morning of December 7, they were listening to Hawaiian tunes on the radio when they saw smoke in the distance. Planes started flying toward them, and they thought the navy was providing an escort. But when a Japanese A6M2 Zero flew up and started in with machine gun fire, they turned back to sea, as they were unarmed. After a while, they made a second effort for a downwind landing at Bellows Field, but as they came onto the runway, they could not stop and careened into a ditch. Just behind them, Zeros came in to strafe the downed plane. Eventually, he was able to exit the aircraft. This native son of South Hill survived what turned out to be the first American air combat of World War II.

Lieutenant Leonard Humiston, U.S. Army Air Corps, in 1940, before the war. Humiston grew up in the Puyallup Heights neighborhood of South Hill and went on to become involved in the first American air battle of World War II. He was later awarded the Silver Star for his actions over New Guinea. *Courtesy of Gene Humiston Cotton.*

Lieutenant Leonard Humiston and his airplane in 1940. *Courtesy of Gene Humiston Cotton.*

# South Hill, Washington

# Letters Home

The South Hill Historical Society was given 143 letters that had been written by Fred Kupfer Jr. during his time serving in World War II. Our thanks go to Michael Kupfer for this generous donation.

The Kupfer family was one of the earliest families to take root on South Hill. Fred Jr. was born February 19, 1908, and was raised in the old Kupfer farmhouse. Fred's father was one of pioneer Alois Kupfer's three sons. Fred's mother was Bessie (Padgett) Kupfer. During World War II, Fred served with the Nineteenth Engineering Battalion, building roads and bridges, as well as setting and clearing minefields. This work put his unit in lead positions with the infantry. His time in the army spanned the duration of America's involvement in World War II in Europe, from December 1942 until Germany surrendered in May 1945.

Letters home, like Fred's, during World War II were highly censored. Any information written home regarding unit location, military exercises or battle situations was strictly censored. Some of Fred's letters even had holes in them, as words had physically been cut from the page by army censors where Fred had inadvertently mentioned names or places that were considered sensitive. With these limitations, the letters were mostly about mundane matters. Often, it was hard for Fred to come up with anything of interest to write about. However, he was diligent, sending letters often that were written very well. Most of his letters were to his mother and father on South Hill and his sister Mary, who worked for the Bonneville Power Office in Portland, Oregon, where she lived. Some of the letters went to his brother Paul and his wife, Gert. Others were sent to a few to his neighbors—familiar names to South Hill old timers—Al Delano (the tavern owner at Willows Corner) and Howard Annis (who worked at the Annis Service Station at Willows Corner).

As mentioned, most letters contained descriptions of the everyday, nonexciting life of a GI (KP, marching, guard duty, et cetera). Fred was thankful for getting the local paper, the *Puyallup Valley Tribune*, cigarettes, camera film and other goodies, including candy, clothing and money (which he indicated he didn't need). Reading the letters, it is clear Fred was not happy with military life; he was homesick and longed for a short war. The rigors of combat were hard on Fred, as he was in his thirties, a bit older than most of his comrades, who were in their teens and early twenties. He even complained of rheumatism. He suffered from episodes of yellow jaundice, bronchial pneumonia and malaria, and he sometimes required hospitalization.

Fred Kupfer Jr., 1942.
*Courtesy of Michael Kupfer.*

Fred completed his basic training at Fort Lewis and engineer training at Fort Leonard Wood, Missouri, a new installation that was only two years old at the time. There, he was taught about bridge building, demolition and mine removal. He was shipped out to England by way of Ireland in September 1942, and he hit the beaches of North Africa that November. Fred was among the first American soldiers to invade North Africa (landing on a beach west of Oran, Algeria), thus beginning America's war against Hitler's Germany and, at that time, their ally Italy.

One of Fred's letters went into detail about his unit's actions in the North African campaign. However, it was written after the battle for North Africa was over, which may have been the reason it was uncensored. Fred wrote that he landed on the beach the morning of November 8, and his unit marched to a brickyard with no resistance; however, they were taking sniper fire where they bivouacked for the night. From there, his unit was ordered to back up the infantry at the front, but they still saw no real action.

Fred's unit made its way deeper into Algeria, sometimes with the infantry. He was in the thick of the famous battle for Kasserine Pass, planting minefields, advancing and retreating under fierce German resistance as Americans tried to enter Tunisia. "This was as close as I came to not making it," he said. After the breakthrough, his unit continued building roads and laying minefields as the Americans pushed the Germans through Tunisia to the coast. His unit built stockades for the thousands of German prisoners. The Germans and Italians surrendered Tunisia in May 1943.

Fred's letters became less frequent after the Americans' rapid march through Sicily and into Italy. Most of his time in the war was spent fighting in Italy. The campaign for Italy was one of the longest and most difficult of the entire war. The Germans were well dug in, using the mountainous terrain to their favor. The Germans gave ground at a high cost to American and Allied troops. The bloody campaign lasted until the last week before Germany's surrender on May 7, 1945.

Fred's letters give us some sense of the progress of that fight. The Americans first entered Italy at the Salerno beaches, approximately two hundred miles south of Rome, on September 9, 1943. Fred's first letter from Italy was dated January 1, 1944, and he wrote that he had had a twenty-two-day stay in the hospital with malaria and yellow jaundice before being put back into the action. "Had a chance to sleep between white sheets and in a bed for the first time in seventeen months."

In a letter dated February 14, 1944, Fred said: "Weather here in Italy miserable. I sure wish that Jerry would start backing up a little faster...there doesn't seem to be any break in sight for us."

> *April 16, 1944:* "Seems like we're always in valleys with the Krauts looking down our throats."
>
> *June 22, 1944:* "I've seen Rome and it's quite a city...am looking forward to seeing the next city… they sure seem tickled to see us. Just to keep you informed, I'm still alive and intend to stay that way after going through almost two years of it."
>
> *July 25, 1944:* "Looks as though Jerry is soon going to be through.... They still are putting up quite a fight here, but we are still making progress."
>
> *November 11, 1944:* "Everywhere were signs welcome to our liberators there is very little that I can write about at this time."

In a letter dated May 11, 1945, four days after the German surrender, Fred gave some details that would have been censored in earlier letters. The following are some highlights. Fred spent the winter of 1944–1945 camped ten miles outside Bologna, Italy; most of his unit's drive through Italy was with the First Armored Division. After entering the Po Valley, they constructed the first American bridge over the Po River, which was used by the Tenth Mountain Division. They had advanced close to the borders of Switzerland and Austria before Germany surrendered on May 7, 1945. His unit was stationed in Belluno, in northern Italy, after the surrender.

Although the war had ended, it took time before they were shipped home. A point system was used to determine departure status (being married with a child was worth twelve points; getting a medal was worth five points; each month in service was worth one point; et cetera). It must have been frustrating to wait months after the surrender to get orders to go back to the United States. Fred left Italy on August 20, 1945. He sent a Western Union telegram home from Camp Miles Standish, Massachusetts, that was dated September 7: "back at last all well here short time then home."

Fred returned to live in Puyallup and worked for the Port of Tacoma for twenty-eight years. Fred died on April 4, 1969, and was survived by his wife, Ruth; two stepdaughters, Mrs. Jeannette Dolph of Puyallup and Mrs. Sally Coyne of Tacoma; both of his parents; his brother, Paul; sister, Mary; and four grandchildren.

## Balloon Bombs

During World War II, the Japanese bombed South Hill. Aerial balloons carried the actual bombs. Those devices were launched in Japan and traveled to this country on the great prevailing west-to-east wind currents at high altitudes, which we now call the jet stream. Timers and barometric switches determined when the balloons would descend and actually explode. Altogether, it is estimated that seven thousand balloons were launched, with some twenty-five hits actually recorded in Washington State. In total, the impact points were scattered all over the West Coast of the United States and Canada, and a few went as far east as Michigan.

There were two bombings on South Hill. One bomb hit on March 3, 1945; it landed on George Barlow's farm, and using today's terminology, it's been determined that it came down a bit west of 94$^{th}$ Avenue, around 134$^{th}$ Street. The Church of Jesus Christ of Latter-Day Saints now sits just a short distance east of the impact point. At that time, 94$^{th}$ Avenue was known as Odens Road.

## South Hill, Washington

Japanese balloon bombs (depicted in this illustration) landed on South Hill during World War II. *Courtesy of Jerry Bates and the South Hill Historical Society.*

In 1945, the Parks family lived near this impact point, and several members of the family still live nearby. Joan Parks Vosler remembers the event well; she was thirteen years old at the time. Her sister, Carol Parks Smith, supported Joan's memory. They recalled that the bomb landed in the late morning. Joan is still certain that she witnessed it coming down. Both sisters remember climbing up an embankment around 94th Avenue and 128th Street and looking south toward the crash point. They could clearly see the white color of the balloon. Their brother, Orin Parks, actually climbed under a fence and went toward the device but was warned to stay away. Sometime thereafter, a contingent of army troops arrived and combed the field by walking across the ground, all in a line, at arm's length. All fragments of the device were picked up and carted away. So far as is known, there were no injuries associated with this event.

Less is known about the landing of the other bomb. In fact, federal records show that only one bomb struck the Hill, and the landing is mentioned in the records of the Smithsonian Institution. We know, however, that an additional bomb did hit. It landed on the Massie farm on March 1, 1945. According to family records, Charles Anion Massie, a local farmer, found it in his apple orchard. His farm was located near present-day Pope Elementary School. He pulled the balloon from an apple tree, cut it apart and gave fragments to each of his children. In 2003, his son Arthur Massie brought his piece to a meeting of the South Hill Historical Society. Arthur Massie has since passed away, but the balloon scrap is still in his family's hands. We are not aware of witnesses to this landing, and there has been no response from military authorities.

## Farm On Stump Alley

### By Helen Heil Rohlman

Our little Heil farm of five acres was purchased in the early 1920s. My dad (Joe Heil) was a widower after his first wife and infant son died during the flu epidemic of that era. He was left with one daughter, Margaret, so they left Chicago and were coaxed out to Washington by acquaintances he knew. My mom (Helena Heil) was divorced and had a daughter, Gertrude. The two of them met in south Tacoma when Dad was working at the Northern Pacific Railroad Shops. They were married on January 31, 1926, and three Heil girls later appeared. First, Dorothy Heil Morris (Seattle), then Mildred Heil Dobbs (Puyallup) and, lastly, yours truly, Helen Heil Rohlman (Alaska).

The folks had it rough during the Great Depression with seven mouths to feed, but they had a cow, pigs, chickens and a large garden, so meat, vegetables and fruit were canned, and even the eggs were preserved by putting them in water glasses. (As I understand, the whole egg was covered in a solution that would seal the pores of the eggshell, and the eggs could be kept longer when the hens ceased laying.)

My mom and dad picked strawberries, raspberries and blackberries every day during the season. They would have an older daughter pick berries with them, and the other would watch the three younger ones. Mom said they made enough money picking berries to buy sugar, flour and other staples to last them through the winter.

Our house was on Walnut Street (now Eighty-Third Avenue East) behind the Fruitland Grange Hall. We girls would laugh and say, "We live on Walnut Street...all the NUTS live there!" Before our road was formally named, it was called Stump Alley because they had to remove about fifty trees and stumps to straighten the road. I believe this was a WPA project so that some men could have a job during the Great Depression. My Dad blasted many of the stumps and used his "buzz saw" to cut the stumps in lengths for our wood stoves.

We had a very small two-story house, and the kids slept upstairs. The only warmth we had was the heat from the wood stoves downstairs when the stair door was propped open. The scariest time of my life was during World War II, as you could hear planes passing overhead, day or night, from McChord Airfield. Our family, like others, had to cover our windows so no light would be evident from above. During that time, it was not unusual to hear a faint rumble in the distance, and it would get louder the closer it came. These were troop convoys from Fort Lewis, Washington, transporting soldiers to the East Auburn Depot (Milwaukee Railroad) for shipment overseas or to other bases. We would run from our home to Airport Road (now 112$^{th}$ Street East) and watch the convoys pass. We would wave and yell "goodbye," not knowing if the troops would return home.

The families on the homefront made small sacrifices, too. Gas rationing, food, meat and sugar stamps were common. Old aluminum pots and pans were donated to the collection center on the island of Broadway and St. Helen's Avenue in Tacoma for the war effort. There were no fresh bananas, just dried ones, and there was no pineapple, coconut or chocolate. Anything good in a cookie was not available. I still remember the Buck Private candy bar that was available during the war years. It seemed to be made of oatmeal, raisins, nuts and molasses with a light carob coating, not a good chocolate coating. There were no tires, no new cars or bicycles—everyone just tightened up their belts and got along.

The best place to live was on a small farm on South Hill because the people were hardworking and could manage to take care of their families.

## South Hill during World War II and the 1940s

### By Barbara Huff Ringo

I enjoyed reading Helen Heil Rohlman's memories. I remember the Heil girls, as they and their mom picked berries at my brother-in-law's berry farm in Puyallup—as did I. We, too, had farm animals and a big garden to feed our large family (seven kids, Mom and Pop and Grandma Whitford) at the reservoir. I have some similar memories.

## A Community History

After the Japanese attack on Pearl Harbor, many things changed. We had to "black out" the windows on the house for one thing. Once, a tank from Fort Lewis got "lost" somehow and ended up at the crossroads of Reservoir Road and Military Road. The "scars" where it turned around were there for years. We had heard it coming up the road and wondered what it could be. The torn-up turf and tread marks gave us the answers. It was quite a thrill to see P-38 airplanes flying above the reservoir when the pilots were getting their flight times. One actually dove toward the reservoir, and I could see the pilot quite clearly. There were Red Cross first aid classes at Firgrove School, where we learned how to bandage wounds and make slings, et cetera. Air raid drills were held as well. Everyone had an emergency route to their homes from school, staying clear of main roads by going through woods and brush to get there.

I belonged to 4-H Club, and one year, I received the Kiwanis Trophy for the best victory garden in Pierce County. My mother, Winnifred Huff, was [the group's] leader then. Later, Florence Glaser (Don's mother), took over as the leader, and I remember going to Achievement Day Rallies at Fruitland Grange Hall. [I also remember] going to Pullman to the 4-H Club camp at Washington State College, where members and leaders from all over Washington attended. That year, my brother Leslie also attended, as did Wayne Glaser and Vernon Rockstad. There was also a 4-H Club camp at Benbow Lake Resort in the summer.

There were lots of social events at Firgrove School—carnivals, Christmas programs, box socials (sometimes called basket socials). The box social was where the women and girls would make picnic lunches and pack them into decorated boxes to be auctioned off to the men and boys and then shared with the successful bidders. This raised money for the school and the PTA. The Christmas programs consisted of plays and entertainment; this was all followed by "Santa" handing out bags of candy, nuts and even oranges.

There weren't many accidents at school, but I remember Billy Stover getting hit by a car or truck in front of the school and getting a broken leg. He lived across [the street] from the school and went home for lunch. Then, when I was in seventh grade, Marlene Rockstad ran behind a batter during a noon recess ball game and was hit by the bat and knocked unconscious. I ran to tell Miss Plank and Mrs. Miller (my cousin), and since there was no ambulance handy or 911 to call, we loaded [Marlene] into Mrs. Miller's car for a trip to Puyallup Clinic to have her cared for. [Her only injury] was a broken front tooth.

Mr. Fred Predmore (Sr.) had a team of horses that my folks hired to come and plow, harrow and later cut and rake the hay for our cows. I always tried to get a ride on the wagon when the hay was picked up to put in our barn, so I could "drive" the horses. In the late 1940s, we had some very cold winters, and once, Don Glaser gave my brother Les, me and his brother a ride in his Model T on the ice on Massey's pond.

In the 1930s and early 1940s, the highway (Meridian) was paved on both sides as far as Mitchell-Gould Road, and from there, only one lane was paved at least as far as Graham. The cars were few in those days, and people would drive on the paved side until another car was seen coming toward them; they would then get over on the unpaved side.

We shopped for groceries at Willows Corner in Miller's store there. Across the road was Annis's Standard Oil Gas Station where we also traded. The other business [in the area] was a tavern run by George Mabbitt.

## The Big C Shingle Mill Company

There were early ventures in manufacturing on the Hill. In the early 1940s, for example, a man named John "Jack" Nicolet started a manufacturing enterprise known as the Big "C" Shingle Mill Company. Jack was born in Tacoma in the early 1890s, but his roots go back to Indiana and, before that, to Switzerland. He moved his family to South Hill in the 1920s and settled near Woodland School. Initially, the family started a chicken farm to produce eggs for sale. Mr. Nicolet, however, had an interest and work history in the wood industry. So, in the early 1940s, he relocated to some acreage on Lunblad Country Road (now Eighty-Sixth Avenue), near what is now Rogers High School. The farm was actually located at the intersection of the Natches Pass Trail (Military Road) and Lunblad Road

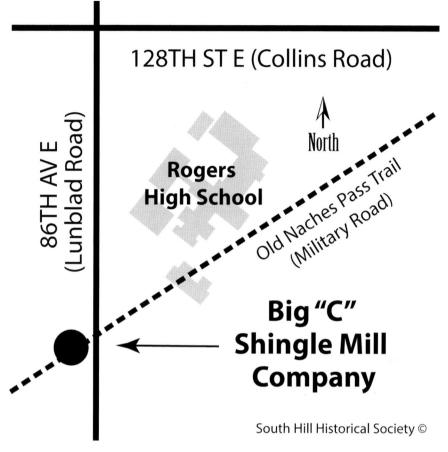

The Big C Shingle Mill Company location. *Courtesy of Jerry Bates and the South Hill Historical Society.*

(at contemporary Glacier Creek Subdivision). It was here that Jack Nicolet started a manufacturing business.

First, he purchased a lease on a section of timber (640 acres) near Ashford, Washington. The agreement restricted timber operations to the cutting and removal of cedar slabs and downed timber. A waterway known as Big Creek ran through most of the section, and Mr. Nicolet named his company for that stream. Using a Cletrac, a type of tractor, the useable timber was first harvested, trimmed and cut into lengths of fifty inches. These were known as "bolts," which were floated down Big Creek to a holding pond. From that pool, they were loaded onto a truck (a Studebaker vehicle, as his son and daughter remember) and moved to South Hill through Elbe and Eatonville.

When the bolts arrived at the factory, they were sawed into sixteen-inch lengths known as "blocks," making them ready for a shingle-producing machine. The blocks were then pushed through a rotating saw on a carriage, thereby producing thin, tapered slices of wood called "shingles." When the carriage was retracted, it would tilt and send the block into the saw again, always producing tapered shingles. Finally, the product went to a clipper-saw, where its edges were trimmed. Shingles were then graded, packed into "bundles" and stacked. At this point, they were ready to sell. One "square" was four bundles, which, when used on a roof, covered approximately ten square feet.

A gasoline engine with a leather belt system was used to power these mechanical operations. A ledger kept by Mr. Nicolet shows that he paid about twenty cents per gallon for gas in the mid-1940s. Mr. Nicolet operated this business through the 1940s.

# Vern Rockstad

Vern Rockstad's family came to Puyallup from North Dakota in 1941 and settled on South Hill, where he enrolled in the Firgrove School for the seventh and eighth grades. He entered Puyallup High School in 1944. He kept busy in the summers by berry picking and working various dairy jobs for Julius Gratzner.

What did youth do for recreation on the Hill during that period? Vern said, "In those days, our winters were much colder, as we all learned to ice skate in the 1940s. There was a small pond below our ten acres, but the best place was Massie's Pond about a half mile southeast of Glaser's. Someone always brought wood to burn in a fifty-five-gallon drum to keep us warm, and we sometimes brought food to prepare."

Vern also participated in 4-H. The Firgrove 4-H club (four for "Head, Heart, Hands, Health") was started in 1929, and it was known then as the Firgrove Potato Raising Club, with over one hundred members and five leaders. Vern joined in 1942. In 1945, the club was in need of a leader. Vern recruited Frank Ballou to lead the club. Frank Ballou who was a well-respected person in the community and so highly thought of that, after his passing, the Puyallup School District named Ballou Junior High after him. Vern told us about the many 4-H activities that he and his friends participated in, including camping at Lake Tanawax and state camps at

Washington State College in Pullman; he said they also participated in the Yakima and Puyallup State Fairs. Vern's blue ribbon–winning pig escaped his captivity at the Puyallup Fair, and for thirty minutes, it led captors on a chase through the fairgrounds. More stories followed. Vern said the South Hill boys were "very creative" when performing skits and brought the house down during county meetings with their operating table scene—pulling pig intestines out of their mock surgical patient.

Vern graduated from Pacific Lutheran College in 1952. "The following day," he said, "three of my best friends and I were sworn into the U.S. Army Security Agency in Seattle during the Korean War. We all served in Germany." After his military service, Vern taught sixth grade at Meeker School. In 1960, he married Jean McDaniel, a third-grade teacher who also taught at Meeker. They both completed their degrees at the University of Washington. He was later hired by the Sumner School District to start their special education programs. Vern taught at Sumner for the next twenty-six years.

## My Early Life on South Hill

### *By Bill Goelzer, March 2004*

My folks both came from the Milwaukee, Wisconsin area. My dad, Lester Goelzer, was born in 1901 and came to Puyallup in 1906. My mom, Faye C. Kehr, was born in 1903 and arrived in Puyallup in 1909. They were married in 1923. When I was born in 1937, a ten-day stay in the hospital cost thirty-five dollars. Dr. Aylen brought us kids into the world at the old Puyallup Hospital. We lived to the west of the Willows Grocery Store in a house my folks had built on ten acres in 1927. The address was Airport Road, Route 2, Box 340. Airport Road (now known as 112$^{th}$ Street/39$^{th}$ Avenue Southwest) had narrow lanes and a water run-off dip on both sides. Drivers were always catching their tires in this groove and throwing their cars every which way.

We had a trail that went through the woods, over a creek and came out next to the Willows Grocery Store. The store was owned by George and Georgia Miller. They had a son, Art, and two daughters, Margaret and Nancy. The girls would sit

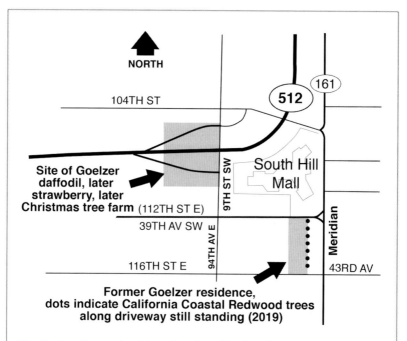

The Goelzer farm and residence locations. The farm is now a freeway interchange. *Courtesy of Jerry Bates and the South Hill Historical Society.*

me on the meat counter and teach me how to tie my shoelaces as they sang, "Billy boy, Billy boy, charming Billy." My older sister, Barbara, and brother, Bob, went to the Puyallup Heights School, with Miss Burns as their teacher. Past the sixth grade, they went to the Puyallup High School. When my younger sister, Georgina, and I started school, we attended Meeker in the Valley. We walked over to the Willows corner to catch the bus. Across the street, where Howard Annis had the gas station, there were lots of willow bushes (Willows Corner). As we all had pocket knives in those days, we would whittle whistles to blow on the bus. The teachers usually took them away when we blew them at school, but we could always make another the next day.

In the 1940s, my sister, brother, Nancy Miller and I went to the McMillan Reservoir on 128th Street (Old Military Road) to have a picnic lunch. At that time, there were picnic tables and lots of lawns [there]. Our dog, Tippy, decided to take a swim in the reservoir, which got us kicked out of there. Sometime after that, they put up fencing and wouldn't let people in the area anymore. I think it was because of the war, not just our dog.

When we needed milk, we would walk over to the Crabb's (who lived on the east side of Meridian) with a couple of empty gallon jugs and we would bring them back full of milk. Bob Crabb had a basketball hoop in the barn, and we enjoyed playing "horse." In the winter, when we had really cold weather, we could ice skate on the frozen creeks. We'd have to stop and crawl through barbed-wire fences so we could skate into the next field.

My dad was a farmer and grew strawberries, daffodils and Christmas trees. We always had a lot of work to do to help our folks. We had over one hundred pickers to harvest the twenty-six acres of strawberries on the farm on Ninth Street, which is now covered with State Road 512, on and off ramps and mini storage sheds. On hot days, my dad would buy four or five cases of soft drinks as a bonus for the pickers. He would also take a pick-up truck load of us up to Five Mile Lake for a swim after work.

My buddies growing up were Martin Crabtree and Willard Bill. They lived where the South Hill Mall is today. The Felbell family along Fifth Street had a large barn, and in the summer, they let us sleep in the hayloft. Sometimes, Mr. Heinz, who lived across Meridian from the McKays' stables, would have us boys stomp down his hay so he could get more into the barn. Then, he'd take us to the Roxie in Puyallup to see Gene Autrey movies. In those days, we had two theaters, the Roxie and the Liberty. The Roxie always showed westerns.

We also hunted with bows and arrows. We would cross Meridian and go east, behind Thackery's and McKay's property. There weren't any roads, but there were trails and a peat bog and lots of swampy areas. We shot a grouse once, built a fire and roasted it. It was kind of raw, but we frontier men ate it anyway. There were trails from Dr. McKay's to the Meridian Riding Club, and we would travel these and explore.

The Millers ran the Willows Store in the 1930s and early 1940s; then the Crabtrees and the Spencers ran the store, and during my high school days in the 1950s, the Letourneaus ran it. Their son, Dick, and I would cashier, stock shelves and handle the business on Sundays by ourselves. My dad passed away in 1975; my older sister and brother passed in 1994; and my mom

passed in 1995. I am lucky that I had wonderful, loving and hardworking parents. My folks' home on 112$^{th}$ Street is gone, but I still live on the back part of the old farm in the home I built in 1961. Huge changes have come to our Hill, with the arrival of the mall, lots of grocery stores, restaurants and traffic. I still like to call the South Hill area my home, and my post office box has a South Hill address. I am glad we have a South Hill Historical Society, and I am proud to be a member of it.

# 7
# THE GRANGE, THE OLD MILL AND THE DRAG STRIP

## *Cultural Roots on the Hill*

In the pre–World War II days, there were few churches and only a few schools on the Hill. Nevertheless, South Hill people did manage to get together in groups and seek governmental action on common problems. School PTAs were very active and served as gathering points. As early as the 1890s, through these types of associations, committees were formed, and petitions were generated for such things as road development and civic improvements.

### THE FRUITLAND GRANGE

At the intersection of 112th Street and 86th Avenue, on the northwest corner, a big barn-like building stands out. It is a common sight to those who commute through the area and shoppers who are traveling to the nearby Costco store. This is the home of the Fruitland Grange. The Grange is a fraternal organization that was created shortly after the Civil War. Initially, the group catered to American farmers, and it was a very powerful political force from the 1890s to the 1950s. Many historians credit the Grange with lobbying for the establishment of rural mail service, the Farm Credit System and other farm-related initiatives of the federal government.

The Fruitland Grange was organized in the spring of 1932, when the aims of two special interest groups came together. One was a very active coalition

The Fruitland Grange, pictured here as it is seen today, was built in 1938. *Courtesy of South Hill Historical Society.*

of citizens called the Woodland Improvement Club. In the early 1930s, it had been successful in securing several significant infrastructure projects on the Hill, but an important one, the establishment of low-priced electricity, had not been realized. It was during this same period that the Washington State Grange was vigorously promoting the efforts of Washington's senator Homer Bone, later known as the Pacific Northwest's father of public power, who was creating legislation for the construction of the Bonneville and Grand Coulee Dams and the production of cheap electric power. The two groups decided to merge, and it was decided that a Grange chapter would be established on South Hill. All of the members of the club elected to move their membership to this new fraternal organization on the Hill.

Thirty-five people participated in the first organizing meeting of the Grange at the Woodland School on April 21, 1932. The installation was administered by a visiting team from the McMillan Grange. The three top officers were selected during this ceremony. Additional officers were elected and installed in May 1932. A ladies' auxiliary was established in 1933. The Grange was formally incorporated in December 1934.

For several years, the Fruitland Lodge operated in the Woodland School. However, in 1938, the old school building was torn down, so from June 1938 to February 1939, meetings were held in the nearby Collins Grange Hall. In 1934, Fruitland purchased land to build its own facility. This was the land on which the current building is located. The first building committee was appointed in March 1935. The Grange began clearing the land in 1936. The Grange Powder Company held a demonstration on the site and blew out most of the tree stumps. Membership labor was then utilized to clear the property.

In March 1936, plans for a proposed hall were accepted. Afterward, in April 1938, a building committee was authorized to borrow $2,500 under terms of the Federal Housing Act. Concrete pouring began on July 8, 1938. The male members of the Grange were there, working with wheelbarrows, while the female Grangers provided food. However, that day's work was just the beginning. Afterward, nearly every Saturday and Sunday, a group of men could be heard hammering away or seen carrying lumber here and there until the main building was completed. At one time, a group of Sumner Grangers came to help. Grangers from other places worked from time to time, helping in various ways. So, the Grange Hall was mostly designed and built with volunteer labor by Grangers from local areas. It was completed in late 1938 and cost $10,000. On February 14, 1939, Grange members held a Valentine dinner in the new hall. This was its first use. The first regular Grange meeting was held on February 17, 1939.

The Fruitland Grange began a Juvenile Grange (Youth Services) in 1939. To support veterans, a program of ward parties was started at Madigan Hospital in 1947. Fruitland has supported little-league baseball on South Hill since 1962. Today, games can often be seen in progress on the Grange site. When infant car seats were first introduced as a safety innovation, the Fruitland Grange pledged $1,155 to the purchase and distribution of fifty-three seats. The club received an award for this program in 1985. Support for the purchase of Thun Field by the county was also once a priority. Many church groups, civic organizations, and educational groups have routinely used the very large Grange Hall for a variety of programs.

## Puyallup Heights Community Club

In the rural setting of South Hill, there slowly evolved some community networks, all of which served to facilitate social interactions and address common problems. These clubs, as they were called, were usually organized around the boundaries of the various school districts of the period. There was, for example, a community club associated with the Woodland School District. Another was linked to the Firgrove School. A third was called the Puyallup Heights Community Club (PHCC).

The Puyallup Heights Community Club was organized on October 9, 1941. It was a replacement for the Puyallup Heights Improvement Club, which had existed since the early 1900s. It was also a replacement for the Puyallup Heights Parent Teachers Association. PHCC did not exactly replace the Improvement Club in all its practices. For years, for example, the old club had been meeting in a hall on Forest Grove School property, but there was concern about this practice. And while PHCC initially held some meetings at the school, it rather quickly shifted to private homes and other locations.

PHCC was never a big organization; its membership averaged between fifteen and twenty people. Other than during the summer, the members got together once a month. The minutes from the organization's meetings show the names of the early Hill residents who were active in its work, including Barth, Goelzer, Kupfer, Abbott, Carlson, Johnson, Yazzolino, Zimmerman and others.

Members of PHCC regularly interacted with personnel at the fire department, the Puyallup School District's PTA, the sheriff's department and other civic organizations. They had particular ties to some fraternal groups, specifically one known as the Improved Order of Redmen, Tribe No. 55. The Redmen Lodge is the oldest fraternal association in the United States, being chartered by Congress and with roots going back to 1765.

As a social force, PHCC was active for some forty years. In the 1940s, members supported the war effort in a number of ways. Civil defense was always an active project. The group's interaction with military personnel included planning dances and other activities. After the war, the group volunteered with service organizations and donated money to charitable groups, such as the Salvation Army, Tacoma Rescue Mission, Red Cross, United Way, March of Dimes, Pierce County Heart Association, American Cancer Institute and others.

In February 1980, PHCC closed its bank account. Donations had stopped, and the bank was assessing a monthly fee. Finally, on January 17, 1984, at the group's last regular meeting, the members who were present voted to disband. The club's total assets of $51.90 were donated to the Tacoma Rescue Mission.

## Frank Ballou

Frank Ballou was a South Hill Community leader with a passion for education. *Courtesy of Bob Ballou.*

Frank and Helen Ballou moved to South Hill in the early 1940s. They settled on a ten-acre ranch just across Meridian Avenue from Firgrove Elementary School. Originally from Des Moines, Iowa, they came to the Puget South region to be near Helen's family, who lived in Puyallup.

When it was acquired, the Ballou property was considered a "stump farm." It was not usable for agriculture and had to be cleared to be of any practical use. Frank used dynamite to blast out the stumps and created areas that could be cultivated. Initially, five acres were devoted to raising strawberries. Over time, the remaining acreage was developed and used for a variety of things, including growing hay, raising raspberries and maintaining normal farm activities and animals.

Soon after his arrival—and because of his agricultural interests—Frank became active in the local Grange. He served for many years in the Fruitland Grange, and by the early 1960s, he had been elected master of the Pomona Grange, an umbrella group for some seventeen Pierce County Granges. For a while, he also served as the deputy master for the Washington State Grange.

Frank helped to establish the annual Pierce County Fair. The fair, now held each year in Graham, was started in 1947 by the Fruitland Grange and was held there for its first two years. It moved to Sumner in 1950, and it remained there for the next eighteen years before relocating to its present site.

In keeping with his agricultural interests, Frank also worked for the State of Washington Employment Service, helping provide farm labor for Pierce County. He was a leader in the 4-H program and was on the board of directors for the Firgrove Water Company.

Frank's second passion was education. Over time, he became active in the Firgrove School PTA, serving as president for a time. In the mid-1950s, he was elected president of the Citizens Committee for Education. This grassroots group was devoted to improving the educational prospects of local students by trying to get better facilities and more qualified teachers. As part of this effort, Frank was credited with being the driving force behind the successful endeavor to move the independent Firgrove School District into the Puyallup School District, thereby providing more opportunities for Hill students.

Frank Ballou died in 1964. In 1971, a new junior high school was built near Frank's old home. In gratitude for his many accomplishments, especially on behalf of education on the Hill, the new school was named in his honor.

## The Women's Benefits Association

The Grange, while it did have a ladies' auxiliary, tended to be mostly gender-oriented and, as such, provided mainly a means for men to congregate and mingle. During the early twentieth century, however, there was one organization that attempted to reach out to South Hill women: the Women's Benefit Association. It was started in 1892 in Port Huron, Michigan, and was aimed specifically at serving rural females and improving their lives by providing benefits and creating places to socialize. The Puyallup-area vehicle for this association was called the Puyallup-Rainier Review, No. 20. "Review" was the name of the local club, a part of a larger state organization.

The minutes and other data from the meetings of this local branch, covering the 1930s, 1940s and part of the 1950s, show that it was an active group. During the 1930s and 1940s, for instance, the membership was large enough to require the rental of a hall each month to accommodate everyone who wanted to participate. That period was apparently the peak era for this local alliance, as data from the 1950s shows that the meetings were then being held in the homes of the various officers.

## Churches on South Hill

### *By Paul Hackett*

Religious worship has always been a priority of the people living on South Hill. Unfortunately, in the early days, the establishment of congregations was difficult. This was primarily due to the distances people had to travel and the light density of the area's population.

## A Community History

Individual families conducted early religious services, but with the growing popularity of automobiles in the early 1900s, many Hill residents began seeking out worship opportunities in other communities, where flocks had already been established. Families of German descent tended to go to Peace Lutheran Church or Immanuel Lutheran Church in Puyallup. Eventually, the establishment of "home" churches became a priority.

Just when the first church was built on the Hill is unknown. The clue we have to such an identification comes from a 1986 Pierce County Planning Department effort, which attempted to locate historic buildings. One finding was a "single-story, wood-frame" building on the northwest corner of 112th Street and 66th Avenue East. It had been identified in 1959 as the Woodland Gospel Temple.

Some church structures were converted from other uses. The Rabbit Farm building at 117th Avenue and 122nd Street was first converted into a store, then to a Sunday school. It became a church in 1948. It was first known as the Highlands Community Church and later as the South Hill Full Gospel Church. Today, it is the Living Hope Church. A number of ministers have been identified as leading this congregation: Pastor Rupp, Reverend Ike Mardock, Reverend Joe Finley and Reverend Joe Finley Jr.

Members of Highlands Community Church (now called Living Hope Church) in the early 1950s, including the Joseph and Muriel Walsworth family and the James and Etta Johnson family. Both families resided in the Rabbit Farms area. *Courtesy of Gail Ostheller.*

Congregants of Shepherd of the Hill Presbyterian Church at a service after they moved into their new building on 112th Street in 1975. Previously, the congregation had worshiped at the Fruitland Grange. *Courtesy of Shepherd of the Hill Presbyterian Church.*

The Hill's Jehovah's Witnesses congregation was started in the Puyallup Valley. A church building was eventually constructed at 113th Street and 78th Avenue. Our Savior Lutheran Church was formed in 1962, after a survey showed a promise of growth. Puyallup Valley Baptist Chapel was originally organized with Omer Hyde, the metropolitan director for the Mount Rainier Association. In 1962, Southern Baptists met in the Hill Funeral Home, and in June 1967, they moved to 79th Avenue and 112th Street. It was subsequently renamed the South Hill Baptist Church. The Firgrove Community Baptist Church was also an outgrowth of a survey. Under the leadership of Reverend Eugene Bartells, the church was incorporated in 1967 and moved into a structure at 136th Street and Meridian Avenue. Later that year, the Presbyterian Church USA appointed Reverend Paul Hackett to organize a church on the Hill. That house of worship, named Shepherd of the Hill Presbyterian Church, met in the Fruitland Grange until a building was constructed at 84th Avenue and 112th Street. Ballou Junior High School once served as a place of worship for the Pilgrim Lutheran Church. That congregation now meets in its own facility at 105th Avenue and 136th Street. As of 2020, there are around twenty-five churches on South Hill.

# A Community History

## Home Craft Club of South Hill

### By Helen Heil Rohlman

The Home Craft Club was formed by a group of ladies who lived in the Woodland School area before and during World War II. From what I can remember, the group held get-togethers about once a month at different ladies' homes. They looked forward to that as much as men looked forward to poker nights out.

Only a few women could drive cars, so the others either walked or hitched a ride to their meetings.

The ladies were interested in new crafts and handiwork and often had projects to complete. One project I remember included each member being asked to bring a large, patterned flour sack and create something out of it. The ideas were numerous; some were made into dishtowels or clothes pin bags and aprons, and someone made a darling little boy's shirt out of one flour sack.

A charitable purpose the group had during World War II was making lap robes for the servicemen at Madigan Hospital in Fort Lewis, Washington. My mom (Helena Heil) spent hours gathering used wool garments, taking the seams out, pulling the loose threads, washing the strips of wool material and then pressing them; she would then cut them in five-inch squares. The final steps were to crochet the edges with bright-colored yarn and then sew the squares in an attractive pattern to make a warm lap cover. The ladies were proud to help with the war effort in any way they could. Some of the Home Craft ladies entered their fancy works into the Puyallup Fair and were quite proud of their accomplishments.

The members I recall are Ann Templin, Nellie Williams, Edna Davidson, Dora Callahan, Mrs Adrain, Virginia Tuttle, Maude Swalander, Erma Goodner and my mom, Helena Heil.

This embroidery was made by Mable Litton of the Home Craft Club on South Hill between the 1930s and 1940s. *Courtesy of South Hill Historical Society.*

# South Hill, Washington

## Romance at the Old Mill Dance Hall

### *By Beverly Olin Brunet, 2007*

It was fifty years ago, and this is what I remember. It was also the most wonderful time of my life, I might add.

On January 12, 1957, I had my first visit to the Old Mill on South Hill. The music was grand, "Good Ole' Fashioned Dance Hall Western Music."

At the time, I was working at the General Telephone Company in Seattle as a draftsperson. Here, I met many local girls from Auburn, Kent and Puyallup. We spent hours primping. Norma, Sandra, MaryLou and I were picked up by Norma's brother at 6:00 p.m. on the dot and were on our way to the "Old Mill." On arrival, the music was playing, and people were just having a wonderful time. It did not take long for nice gentlemen to ask us to dance. Oh, the music was great—good old western music. We never sat down the whole night. There were soldiers from Fort Lewis and airmen from McChord Air Force Base. There were many more guys than girls.

Along came the most handsome man I had ever seen in my life, and he asked me to dance. He was so polite that he called me "ma'am." He told me he was from California. Well,

The Old Mill Dance Hall played "Good Ole' Fashioned Dance Hall Western Music" in the 1950s. *Illustration courtesy of Jerry Bates.*

I thought everyone from California was a movie star. His name was Jack. As I think back, "movie star" must have meant "really handsome" to me. I only danced one dance with Jack that night. I kept looking for him, but there were so many dances and so many men to dance with that I lost track of him. When the dance was over, we girls got back into the car and headed for home, but we were hungry, so we stopped at the "Mint Cafe" on Cole Street in Enumclaw for a much-deserved hamburger, fries and a shake. Let me tell you, after all that dancing, our curly hair was straight, our makeup sweated away, we had grit in our mouth and even our teeth were dirty from the sawdust we had ground up on the dance floor. I think we wore out our shoes, too. Luckily, we had Sunday to recuperate because [we had to be at work at 7:00 a.m.] on Monday.

As our food was being served, guess who walked through the door. It was Jack. There he was again, smiling at me with these perfect white teeth, coal-black hair, nice casual suitcoat, just as neat as a pin. I thought to myself, "I look awful—too late now." He took a seat beside me and pinned me in the booth. He had some buddies with him, and we all talked until the early morning hours. I gave him my name, address and telephone number. (I still have the paper that I wrote it on.)

The next Saturday night, we girls headed for the Old Mill to do it all over again. I sat in the canteen at the Old Mill for a little while, waiting for my special guy (Jack) to come through the door. Then, all of a sudden, I saw another guy who was even more handsome than Jack. He had coal-black hair and a light aqua-colored jacket. I said to myself, "To heck with that guy I met last week. I am going to go out of my way to meet this guy." As I nonchalantly moved toward him, he turned, smiled and, to my surprise, he just happened to be named Jack also. He politely asked me to dance. Infatuated and googly-eyed, I accepted.

While we were dancing, I smelled something just awful. It was a very bad smell. I wanted to get away from him, away from that smell, so I excused myself to go to the restroom. In the restroom, there was plenty of commotion. The girls were wiping mustard off their sweaters and dresses. I did not have any mustard on me, so I began helping the other girls. It was so funny, and everyone was laughing. I emerged from the restroom laughing so hard that it made my stomach hurt. Outside, Jack was waiting for me. He took my hand, and we started to dance. Then Norma asked, "My gosh, what is all over his jacket?" He turned around and the whole back of his jacket was covered with stinky mustard. Every person we had bumped into on the dance floor had mustard on them. Rumor has it that some girl was mad because I had stolen her boyfriend. I am guessing that when we had danced past the canteen, she had squeezed a whole container of mustard on the back of Jack's coat. From that day forward, Jack was called "Mustard" within our circle of friends.

As time went on, the number of girls going to the Old Mill increased from four to ten. My uncle Ed Pierce had moved to Seattle. He had an old 1949 GMC Suburban. He was a very trusting person and told me that I could use the truck on Saturday night to go to the Old Mill. His daughter, my cousin Rondella, wanted to go, too. I had to travel on the metropolitan bus out to Alki Avenue, pick up the Suburban and drive all over Seattle to pick up the ten girls. We sang songs and just had the greatest time driving out to Puyallup. Mary Lou was scared to ride over the railroad tracks. We had to drive over one set of railroad tracks to get to the dance. When we crossed the railroad tracks, she always closed her eyes, kicked her legs and screamed. We always laughed. The tracks were a sign that we were getting close to the Old Mill. The excitement mounted, and we rolled down the windows, bursting out in unison, singing, "Give us some men who are stout-hearted men"—and so on. (This song was sung by Nelson Eddy in the musical *Stouthearted Men* with Jeanette McDonald.) We would arrive at the dance, meet our boyfriends and dance all night.

Sometimes, we would get to the dance early just so we could all get a chance to dance with one special guy we called "Little Elvis." It was only safe to dance with him before his other fan club arrived (on motorcycles). When they arrived, we faded into the woodwork. Boy, that kid could really do the "Bop."

Somewhere in this memoir, I must write about the music and the dance. There was a song the band played called "Pink Cadillac." It was probably a two-step. There was a drum crescendo, which turned into a tom-tom sort of beat. Everyone was bopping and stomping the floor in rhythm to the drum.

# A Community History

> This dance was called the "Old Mill STOMP." The drummer would play the same beat for about four minutes and then instantly stop—the entire band was silent. Everyone just kept dancing to the beat, and that building rocked on its foundation. Believe me, it was a test of endurance. You never knew when the band was going to fire up again. No matter how long it took, no matter how long we stomped, no one ever got out of step. It was a sight to see.
>
> Jack and I continued to go to the "Old Mill" almost every Saturday night. Since neither of us had a car and he was stationed at Fort Lewis and I lived in Seattle, it was the only way we could see each other. In October, Jack went on leave to his hometown in San Fernando, California, and brought back a 1952 Dodge. Then he would come to see me on Sunday.
>
> On October 31, 1957, on our way home from the Old Mill, Jack asked me to marry him. We never went to the Old Mill again. We were married on December 28, 1957, at St. James Cathedral in Seattle (in the chapel). After he was discharged from the army on July 7, 1958, we moved to San Fernando, where we stayed until 1977. We then moved to Redding, California, where I still live. We had five children—four boys and one girl. My beautiful, handsome Jack passed away on December 20, 1993.
>
> Four of us married the men we met at the Old Mill in Puyallup.

## The Puyallup Dragway

The present-day crossroads of 160th Street and Meridian Avenue lives in the memory of the thousands of racing fans who came there from all over the Northwest in the 1960s and 1970s. At that time, Thun Field was an established small airport, and in 1960, racing enthusiasts built an automobile drag strip parallel to the Thun Field runway, between the runway and 110th Avenue. It was known alternately as the Puyallup International Dragway, the Puyallup Raceway Park and the Puyallup Valley Raceways, though the site was not in the valley.

The 1961, Puyallup Valley Raceways' yearbook described the year-old facility:

## South Hill, Washington

*The Puyallup Valley Raceways, built in 1960, is the most modern sanctioned 1320 strip in the Northwest. Over 90 acres of land were cleared and some 70,000 yards of earth moved before it was completed. The track consists of 5,820 feet of paved area and is 60 feet wide, with an additional 15 foot shoulder on each side. Besides the quarter mile for actual racing, there is a 400 foot staging area and a 4,100 foot shut-off area. For the participants, there are 20 acres of pit area, and it gives them plenty of room to work on their cars. Included in this 20 acres is a check-in area, where the cars are divided into specific classes and safety-checked. The viewers have 40 acres of parking area. Both the starting and finishing lines can be seen by those who wish to remain in their cars. Night racing is a feature of the Puyallup Valley Raceways, as the strip is completely lighted. A public address system is utilized at all times to inform everyone present of the speeds and elapsed times of the contestants. Puyallup Valley Raceways is the result of over $150,000 spent in an effort to provide viewers and participants with the best racing facilities available.*

The drag strip was both loved and hated. While it was exceptionally well-liked by racing enthusiasts, it was despised by some local residents. Noise was a big complaint. The facilities were not adequate to accommodate crowds. Parking was always a problem. The local roads were jammed during meets, requiring sheriff's deputies to focus on the area and keep a presence to ensure

The drag strip at Thun Field was a popular and controversial attraction on the Hill in the 1970s. *Courtesy of Joan Vosler.*

## A Community History

*Top*: A car, a crowd and 1,320 feet of pavement at the Puyallup Dragway in the 1960s. *Photograph by George Haskett, courtesy of the Puyallup Dragway Facebook page.*

*Bottom*: A dragway race promotion. *Dick Page Collection, courtesy of Puyallup Dragway Facebook page.*

that law and order was maintained. Toilet facilities were so limited that health problems were a concern, and local residents were always complaining about the sanitation behavior of the people who attended races.

In 1971, the county attempted to bring things under control. The operators of the drag strip proposed to improve the property but also wanted to add a motorcycle track to the complex. (Sunrise Village Shopping Center now occupies the area that was the motorcycle addition.) The county approved the plan but imposed a number of conditions to which the operators had to conform in order to keep their permits. The mandates included noise control, fencing, crowd control and more.

The county's actions apparently doomed the racing center. Subsequent yearly inspections noted that the directed requirements were not being adequately addressed. In 1979, for example, an inspection reported that the tracks were in a state of disrepair and apparently unused. Local residents suggest that the race track stopped formal operations in September 1978.

# South Hill, Washington

## Fred the Barber

### *By Debbie Burtnett*

For decades, Fred Gendreau has been "Fred the barber" to South Hill residents. To his daughter, Leah, he was a celebrity while she was growing up. "It was hilarious to go anywhere with Dad in town...*everybody* knew him! When I was growing up, kids would always say, 'Wow, your dad is Fred the Barber?'"

Fred did not foresee a career in the service industry at age thirteen, when he was a shoeshine boy at Floyd's Barbershop in Puyallup. Born and raised in Puyallup, Fred lived near the current site of Good Samaritan Hospital on five acres of land, and he raised his family of four children with his wife, Sandra, for fifty-nine years on the same piece of property.

Fred had no "ambition" for becoming a barber. He happened to be reading a poster at a vocational school one day and ended up in the barber's program. An instructor approached him. "You can start in that class tomorrow if you want." Sandi Gendreau said, "Fred came from a family of eight, lived in a tiny little house on 7th Street by Good Sam, and he was second to the youngest....His mom was saying, 'You've got to do something!'" He ended up going to Bates Vocational School, where he saw the barber poster. Thus, Fred began his training commenting, "Funny when life takes you that way."

Fred used his training while serving in the navy reserves from 1964 to 1966. Although he asked for a more exotic posting, Fred ended up stationed in the tide flats in Tacoma and was able to barber both aboard his ship and in the area. While at sea, he was always seasick, so the home base was a blessing. "I had a lot of good friends who went to Vietnam and never came back," Fred recalled.

Once out of the service, Fred returned to Kenny Day's old-time barbershop in Puyallup full time. He married Sandra Inman, and they became parents to four children—Stacey, Fred, Sarah and Leah. Kenny Day's shop was first located on Meridian Avenue, next to the railroad tracks, but the shop moved to a location behind the Puyallup Safeway Grocery Store. It was there that Fred heard from his customers. "As I talked to my customers, they kept saying how much they hated to come all the way down the Hill to get services," explained Fred. "I heard more and more of that, so I thought that I'd go there and meet them and be in their neighborhood....That's how I decided to start the first shop."

## A Community History

Fred borrowed $500 from his parents to start his own business. To repay that money, he had to earn $20 per day while barbering to cover the mortgage for the house and the business. There were many days when he didn't make his personal "quota." While starting a business was a "scary thing to do," it grew profitably, and Fred bought more property to build a larger shop and a suite of offices. Sandi Gendreau commented, "It's rare for a free-standing business to last as long as Fred's has for over forty years." Fred said:

> *When I came up the road to start the business, Moreland Tree Farms occupied the place where the mall is today....To the South was Willows Corner, where a tavern and a couple of little stores were located. I set up shop on 128$^{th}$ in a small room adjacent to a little gas station plus feed store....Everything that was in between and farther out was trees, although Firgrove School was there. There were no stores of any kind until you came to the Willows.*

He recalled how quickly the Hill began to develop. Citing the locations of Kentucky Fried Chicken, Pep Boys and Schucks, Fred said a friend of his father's owned the land and offered to sell it for $23,000, but he said, "I couldn't do it, even though I knew development was going to happen. Over a period of fifteen years, the property escalated in value until it was sold for $480,000."

The original five-hundred-square-foot shop—for which Fred purchased land and built—remains on the Hill near Good Sam as a remodeled home for Sandi's mother. Once it was moved from the 12303 123$^{rd}$ Street address to 5$^{th}$ Street, near the hospital, he said, "Then I had the empty lot and built a 10,000-square-foot office building on that same location—12303 Meridian Avenue East—while living in a white house where Big Foot Java is now located. It took about a year—then we got the building going."

Fred and family have contributed a lot to the Hill in terms of their volunteering. For almost ten years, they fostered eight children, "knowing they'd be adopted" and sponsored two Vietnamese families (who went to school and started an orthodontic clinic in Puyallup). Fred was a "big brother"—to help young boys without dads—and supported Rogers High School through his business with basketball calendars, donations to cheerleading squad, yearbook advertisements and free haircuts for students. His shop provided gift baskets for auctions and offered other free services. He sponsored Fred & Company baseball little-league teams and one for the "big guys" through the recreation division of the YMCA. Fred also gave

From a five-hundred-square-foot barbershop to a ten-thousand-square-foot office building, "Fred the Barber" cut hair on South Hill for over forty years. *Courtesy of South Hill Historical Society.*

The House of Kee is a popular restaurant and night club that was established in 1982 at the corner of 152$^{nd}$ Street and Meridian Avenue. It has the distinction of being the Hill's oldest ethnic eating place. Chinese American restaurateur Peter Kee and his wife, Shirley, were the initial proprietors, and the business is still family-owned and operated. Peter is proud of the contribution that he and his family have made to the community of South Hill. *Courtesy of South Hill Historical Society.*

back to the community by making house calls for homebound customers (for no charge), taking homemade soup in Tupperware to his elderly clients.

In 2013, Fred was still working three days a week. Of his client base, Fred said, "I still have clients I first cut in 1965 and have served several generations of the same family…children, grandchildren and now great-grandchildren, as well as older customers like 'Glenn,' who graduated PHS in 1930—I still cut his hair, but at his home." His other notable customers have included Dr. Hilliard and wife, Connie, who built Northwest Trek.

Fred takes great pride in his shop and its management over the decades, having employed as many as eight barbers over the years—four of these barbers working for him for twenty-five years or longer. Fred said they are "really great people."

Fred turned the business over to Chantel Waterbury, which ensured both tenancy and consistency in Fred & Company's service. "She took over the entire shop, quite a few employees, and she's doing fine," bragged Fred.

## Pete and Linda Ziemke and the Garden of Eden

When Wisconsinite Pete Ziemke first visited Washington State to see his mother and brothers—who had come west years earlier—he recalled, "I had one hundred dollars in my pocket, the clothes on my back and two suitcases." Shortly after arriving, he threw away his round-trip ticket. He later married a South Hill girl named Linda and fulfilled his dream—he found a place to live with space for an attached retail nursery.

Pete had a background in landscaping. "I loved working with nature and playing in the dirt," he said. So, after they were married, he and Linda started looking for a home with adjacent land for a nursery site. After a long, frustrating search, they discovered a house for sale on two and a half acres along Shaw Road. His wife thought it was too far out and unsafe, as it didn't have streetlights, but Pete saw the surrounding area as prime land for future housing developments—just what a new nursery business would need. They made an offer on the house with only one concern—they needed more land. The owner offered six more acres, and a deal was made.

Shortly after that, in 1977, the Garden of Eden Nursery was opened. They started on a shoestring while Linda worked at Good Sam Hospital, and the nursery was only open on weekends. "We tried everything to make a buck," said Pete, "including selling Rhododendrons out of the

The Garden of Eden Nursery is nestled along Shaw Road as it climbs the Hill (1977–2001). *Courtesy of Pete Ziemke.*

back of the pickup truck parked along Meridian [Avenue] and locations in downtown Puyallup."

After building up nursery stock, Pete worked at his business seven days a week. He said, "105 hours a week was typical for me, not rare—typical!...I never felt it was work because I loved what I did, and we met so many wonderful people along the journey." He added, "With new developments going in all around us, one after another, such as Manorwood and Crystal Ridge, business was good."

Pete started stringing Christmas lights at the nursery. First, he put a few strings up that his father-in-law had given him, adding more each year. It grew into quite a light show. "It attracted people from miles around," Pete recalled. The Garden of Eden Nursery's Christmas lights attracted a very famous visitor one Christmas Eve, Reverend Billy Graham. Pete had done work for Mr. Graham's youngest son who lived on Lake Tapps, when a windstorm and falling cedar tree caused severe damage to Ned Graham's home. Ned, a grateful customer, became a friend and told Pete that if he could ever do him a favor in the future, to let him know. On hearing this, Pete extended an invitation to Ned Graham's famous father to someday visit "another" Garden of Eden at Christmas time. So, Billy Graham, his wife, Ruth, and their grandchildren came calling. Pete is proud of his Viking heritage, and most of his friends call him the "Viking." On being introduced to his famous visitor, Pete asked Mr. Graham if he should call him Reverend, Doctor or Pastor Billy Graham. Mr. Graham asked, "Can I call you Viking?" Pete said yes, and Graham replied, "You can call me Billy." As pictures were being taken afterward, Billy Graham said, "I've been photographed with many people—world leaders, movie stars, sports stars, but never a Viking!" Pete said, "He was a truly humble man."

Garden of Eden Nursery continued to operate until 2001.

# 8
# DEVELOPMENT

After World War II, extensive development began on the Hill. From 1940 to the mid-1970s, the number of households on South Hill grew by about 150 percent. Seeing the ever-growing demand for housing on the Hill, developers responded, building even more and more housing tracts. Unfortunately, job opportunities on the Hill did not increase in proportion to the influx of people. As a result, many workers were forced to travel the existing roads to jobs in Tacoma, Seattle and elsewhere. The 1972 completion of State Route 512, a four-lane highway that cut across Puyallup Heights and Woodland, helped facilitate thousands of daily commutes to and from the Hill.

By the early 1980s, South Hill was seen by some local government leaders as a worthy destination for large industries. Fairchild Semiconductor Corporation opened a large chip manufacturing plant near Thirty-Ninth Avenue Southwest in 1981. Fairchild sold the plant to National Semiconductor six years later, but semiconductor work was short-lived on the Hill.

Commercial manufacturing never took root on South Hill, but housing growth continued. Today, South Hill is covered with housing developments. They range in size from very large planned communities, such as Gem Heights and Silver Creek, Sunrise and Manorwood, to smaller groupings, such as mobile home parks and apartment buildings. Each can be considered an individual community, existing within the overall boundaries of South Hill. Some are decades old, while others were built recently.

# A Community History

## Planning in the Sixties and Seventies

In the early years of its settlement, South Hill was primarily an agrarian area. During those times, groups like the Grange, PTA and community clubs served as community development initiators. Their meetings brought together the local people for social affairs and discussions about various community needs. Civic projects, from early road development to the establishment of water sources, can be credited to the initiative of these grassroots citizen groups. From the 1890s through the 1940s, this kind of community development worked well. But as time passed and the population grew, more and more people became concerned about the Hill losing its character and quality of life. As the number of people increased, residents increasingly had to turn to the government to initiate community services. However, even given the necessity for their reliance on local officials, residents on the Hill still had a strong belief that they knew what was good for their community.

South Hill experienced major changes in the 1960s. This transformation was convincingly brought to the attention of Reverend Paul Hackett, who arrived on South Hill in 1967. He had been sent to the area by the United Presbyterian Church to start a new congregation, as he had spent the previous several years in Saudi Arabia, pastoring to workers in the petroleum industry. His ecclesiastical efforts were eventually successful, leading to the formation of Shepherd of the Hill Presbyterian Church. It is still a viable local institution. Paul clearly remembers his early impressions of South Hill. He found that the mix of people living on South Hill was in transition. It was changing from an area devoted to farming to more of a concentrated suburban community. Many of the people he first encountered were rooted in the old rural lifestyle, and their thinking reflected that background. Yet, he noted that there was also a steady influx of newcomers who had different points of view on the world. These differing assessments posed a challenge to a member of the clergy, who wanted to serve the entire community.

To find common ground and to bridge the gap between groups, Paul and several others set about creating a community-wide, grassroots action organization known as the Township 19A Association (T19A). The name was derived from the fact that all of South Hill was within the boundaries of Township 19, the Hill's official federal designator. It was a group of about two hundred concerned people. Its stated purpose was "to improve the total environment of Township 19 community by conservation and development of her natural, manmade and human resources."

# South Hill, Washington

# A Community History

*Opposite, top*: An aerial view of South Hill in January 1972, looking north from the intersection of 116th Street East (present-day 43rd Avenue) and Meridian Avenue toward a mobile home park, Willows Corner (112th Street East and Meridian Avenue), and the Puyallup Valley below. This photograph was ordered by Puget Sound National Bank. *Courtesy of Tacoma Public Library, Richards Studio Collection, D161273-4.*

*Opposite, bottom*: An April 3, 1973 aerial view of South Hill looking south down Meridian Avenue. The construction of Highway 512 was underway, as shown at the lower right corner of this photograph. Much of South Hill remained undeveloped, but signs of growth included the increased traffic on Meridian Avenue. This photograph was ordered by Collison Realty. *Courtesy of Tacoma Public Library, Richards Studio Collection, D163161-3.*

*Above*: The "Gingko" model home in the Forest Green development on South Hill, built by Crest Builders as one of the two homes constructed on permanent locations as part of the 1970 Tacoma Home Show. The Gingko home was listed for $18,150 and featured two bedrooms, rough-sawn siding, underground utilities, a green front door and a greenbelt that ran behind each home in Forest Green. To attract potential homebuyers, Forest Green's grand opening occurred during the home show. This photograph was ordered by Homebuilders Association of Greater Tacoma. *Courtesy of Tacoma Public Library, Richards Studio Collection, D15797111-C.*

T-19-A was started in February 1969 by an initial group of about fifty people under Hackett's leadership. During its preliminary meetings, the group developed bylaws and selected the area to be included in the organization's base. To facilitate communications, they started a newsletter. Subsequently, it built relationships with the Washington State Patrol for traffic safety. It contacted the University of Washington, which eventually provided a part-time planner to help. It cemented an operational rapport with the South Hill Athletic Association and with the University of Puget Sound. And, significantly, it cultivated a working relationship with the Puyallup Chamber of Commerce. It regularly coordinated its activities with county officials.

Members of T-19-A labored for about two years on the outline of a community development concept for South Hill. Their most significant accomplishment was probably an agreement to survey the citizens of South Hill regarding their desires for the community. Unfortunately, by 1972, the body of T-19-A had started to fragment. It eventually disappeared; however, the developed concepts survived and were subsequently used by other community leaders.

## The South Hill Community Development Organization

Soon, the South Hill Community Development Organization picked up where T-19-A had left off. The core group of people who were starting the South Hill Community Development Organization had also been members of the original T-19-A. They chose to carry on some of the plans and activities of their past union. One of the more important tasks they continued was the completion of a questionnaire for surveying the citizens of South Hill. The idea was to determine a profile of the community and ascertain what kind of future development the people desired.

The community survey was completed in March 1972. Around 150 volunteers did the work. A total of 1,532 households were targeted. The questionnaires were eventually completed by 1,112 of these family units. Since each unit consisted of several people, the total population count was 4,362. About 7,000 people lived on the Hill at the time, so the number of those who represented in the responses comprised more than half of the total population.

## He Didn't Know a Two-by-Four from a Two-by-Six

### By Jerry Bates

My history of living on South Hill goes back to the late 1960s, when our family moved to the Hill from Puyallup, into a new development "way out" on 128th Street. My early years on the Hill—1968 through about 1985—were filled with great memories of a different South Hill. I think of this period as "suburbia, stage one." The existing businesses and new ones that were popping up along Meridian Avenue were still family-owned, small operations—restaurants, service stations, video stores, taverns, dentists, barbershops, beauty salons, shoe repair shops, et cetera. Most would all give way, in short order, to large corporate-owned chains and franchises.

When I think back, I recall the frustration of having to drive to Tacoma or Puyallup to do serious shopping at a "big" store, such as Sears, J.C. Penney, Bon Marche (remember the Bon), et cetera. But for weekend carpenters, "closeness" was more important than "bigness." I was like many others on the Hill back in the 1970s and 1980s who were either building or remodeling their homes. If you needed lumber or ran out of nails, the choice was between the new place called South Hill Lumber or the well-established Willows Lumber—that was it. Not a weekend would go by that you wouldn't find me at one or the other, but most of the time it was Willows Lumber.

I hear over and over again from our members the fond memories of Willows Lumber—the homemade peanut brittle, the friendly store employees. It was the hub of social activity, a place where neighbors ran into each other and a friendly chat would follow. It's a laid-back environment missing in today's "big box" stores, where you're lucky to see a familiar face along the endless aisles. Maybelle Hoenhous and her late husband, Chuck, ran Willows Lumber for forty-five years. After serving in World War II, Chuck became an insurance salesman and later worked for St. Regis. Chuck and Maybelle (or "Grandma May" as she is used to hearing nowadays), moved to Puyallup in 1945. Maybelle recalled, "As far as South Hill is concerned, about the only thing I remember was we had to go through it to get to Lake Kapowsin, where we fished—it just seemed like it was all woods."

In 1950, Arnold Christianson, the president of C&E Lumber in Randle, Washington, offered Chuck a job running their new lumber outlet on South Hill, a facility owned by Al Delano, who was also owner of Willow's Tavern. Chuck took the offer. He said he "didn't know a two-by-four from a two-by-six but liked meeting new people." Fortunately, Maybelle's father was a carpenter, and Chuck was a fast learner.

Willows Lumber started as a small operation on the south side of Meridian Avenue; in the beginning, it was just Chuck, a truck driver and Maybelle, who would do the books at night. Chuck worked the lumberyard himself, without the aid of a forklift. Business grew when local mink farmers and homebuilders became good customers. During that era, Chuck and Maybelle's sons, Al and Joe, played in the woods and fields behind the store. The boys grew up as the lumberyard grew, "piece by piece by piece," said Alan. Chuck and Maybelle built a house on 132$^{nd}$ Street, bordering the Starkel Turkey Farm. One morning, Alan remembered finding their yard full of a thousand turkeys that had escaped from a hole that had been left in the fence by poachers the night before. "How to herd so many birds back into the farm?" Alan wondered aloud. "Simple," said Mr. Starkel, "you just walk, and they follow." They walked up the road, escorting a thousand turkeys through the farmyard gate. "The turkeys joined their friends," commented Alan.

The business continued to grow, and it became the sole distributor for treated lumber that was used for pole-built barns. They delivered

The Willows Lumber Company, pictured here when the main store was located on the south side of 112$^{th}$ Street East in the 1960s and early 1970s. *Courtesy of Maybelle Hoenhouse.*

the treated lumber all over Washington State and sometimes went into Idaho and Oregon. In the 1960s, they purchased land across the street and started a U-Cart Cement business. Customers could haul home variously sized loads of cement in specially designed trailers attached to their vehicle.

In 1970, Chuck and May became part owners in the Willows Lumber Company, and Charles Jr. (Joe) became involved in the growing business. In 1974, Willows Lumber Company bought the Reynolds' Grocery Store that was across the street and next to the U-Cart operation. The former grocery store site allowed for expansion. The previous lumber store on the other side of the street became a nursery and craft store managed by Chuck and May's son Al, Al's wife, Linda, and Joe's wife, Rhoda. They all worked there until they started their own families, and in 1979, the property was leased to various businesses. In 1993, they sold the property to U.S. Bank. The business continued to grow, and the number of employees, both full- and part-time, grew to thirty. In 1980, Chuck retired, and Maybelle and her sons began running the businesses.

From 1985 to 1987, agents were buying up land for the future South Hill Mall. The property that was needed for the mall included the Willows Lumber Store on the north side of 112th Street. The Hoenhouses sold the property in 1987, and Willow's Lumber had to find a new home. Maybelle said, in hindsight, that "this would have been the time to quit the business," but they wanted to continue for the sake of their sons and loyal employees. That same year, they leased and moved to the O'Leary property on 98th Street (this section of 98th Street no longer exists), just north of what was then Norm's Auto Wrecking, at the corner of 98th Avenue and 112th Street.

In 1991, Willows Lumber had to move again. The mall expanded, buying the O'Leary land, to make room for a new Sears store. Fortunately, at this time, a new opportunity became available on Canyon Road—the former Custom Kraft store and land were for sale. Willows Lumber moved its operations to this new site, but problems arose. The Hoenhouses encountered continual frustrations with changing Pierce County codes and permit requirements, in addition to banking issues. Also, a competing McLendon's Hardware Store was built nearby. The emergence of the "big box" home centers, such as Home Depot and Lowes, meant that times were changing for small, family-run businesses. Faced with all these obstacles, it was time to call

Puyallup School District superintendent and Kiwanis District lieutenant governor Tom Terjesen presents the charter for the South Hill Sunrisers Kiwanis Club to Chuck Hoenhous during a banquet at Ivan's Restaurant in Puyallup on October 28, 1972. *Courtesy of Sunrisers Kiwanis Collection.*

it quits. In 1995, an auction was held, and Maybelle closed the doors of Willows Lumber for the last time.

Chuck Hoenhous gave a lot of his time to civic activities and improving his community. He was the president of the Puyallup High School PTA and served on the Puyallup School Board for twelve years, from 1954 to 1966, presenting all three of his children with their high school diplomas. In addition, Chuck was the first president of the Sunrisers South Hill Kiwanis Club and served on the Ezra Meeker Historical Society board. In his later years, Chuck was known for his "Dad's Peanut Brittle," which was sold at local farmers' markets. The Hoenhouses definitely left their mark on South Hill and in the memories of those of us who fondly recall Willows Lumber and the days of a more home-grown business environment on the Hill.

Chuck passed away on June 9, 2012, at the age of ninety-three. He is survived by Maybelle, Joe and Alan, and his daughter, Pat Smith of Belfair, Washington.

## A Community History

The obtained data established a fact that the Hill was no longer populated by small farms and people living off the land; 37 percent of the heads of households, for example, described themselves as being professionals, technical workers, holding management positions and the like. Another 25 percent declared they were craftsmen. Other data also showed that South Hill had become a bedroom community. It was revealed, for example, that residents mostly commuted to jobs in nearby communities: Tacoma (32 percent), Puyallup/Sumner (13 percent), Seattle (6 percent) and other neighboring locations. Only 6 percent of the respondents stated that they worked on South Hill. When asked how many years each family had lived on South Hill, 45 percent responded that they had been there for less than ten years. Only 2 percent declared a residency of more than forty years (i.e., from the 1930s); 53 percent had been at their then-current address for five years or less. Only 1 percent had been living at the same location for four decades or more. Each respondent was also asked about their shopping habits. The data revealed that 42 percent bought gasoline on South Hill or in Summit; another 38 percent filled up in Puyallup. When buying groceries, 67 percent went to Puyallup, while only 11 percent bought on South Hill; another 11 percent shopped in Tacoma. When purchasing clothing, 54 percent went to Tacoma and another 36 percent to Puyallup. No one purchased on South Hill. To procure building materials, 48 percent journeyed to Puyallup, 27 percent stayed on South Hill or in Summit and another 17 percent traveled to Tacoma.

So, by the early 1970s, South Hill was beginning to take on the demographic profile that eventually formed the present-day community. The residents were mostly newcomers who worked off the Hill. And since this was prior to the arrival of the South Hill Mall and the strip malls along Meridian Avenue, residents did their shopping principally in Puyallup and Tacoma.

Respondents thought that mobile homes should be restricted to mobile home parks and subdivisions where lots were purchased. It was the opinion of 53 percent of respondents that neighborhood streets should not be extended to main arterials. About one-third thought that subdivisions should be either of a cluster design or some type of cul-de-sac, and 81 percent wanted small farms to be a part of the land use mix. A need for parks was also expressed. About one-third wanted a community park developed, while about one-fourth thought it should be either a neighborhood design or some combination approach.

When asked who should have the most influence on the development of South Hill, 67 percent thought it should be residents and community groups. Only about one-third indicated happiness with their governmental representative; 36 percent declared that they were fairly dissatisfied or very dissatisfied. As for possible annexation or incorporation, respondents wanted no part of it; 54 percent said no.

In summary, three quarters (76 percent) envisioned a South Hill that would be a suburban residential area, where people commuted to work elsewhere and to shop and a place where development was clustered in groups, with undeveloped land between the clusters.

## The South Hill Economy in the Late 1970s

In July 1977, the Department of Economics at the University of Puget Sound published a report titled "An Economic Study of the Puyallup Valley–South Hill Area of Pierce County, Washington." The authors were Ernest Combs, Bruce Mann and Michael Veseth, and the work was funded by the Pierce County Planning Department to develop basic background information for county planners. The authors found that, during the period between 1960 and the 1970s, both Washington State and Pierce County had grown more rapidly than the national average. The growth rate appeared to be about 3.5 percent per year. They also concluded that the in-migration population was largely composed of young families and school-aged children. The study determined that most people were employed outside of the neighborhoods where they lived and that the Puyallup Valley–South Hill area operated as a suburban residential region for the rest of the county. Retail stores and contract construction comprised the bulk of local employment opportunities. In terms of jobs held by local residents, most were of the blue-collar type.

Citizens in the area in 1977 considered housing a challenge. The report stated that, from 1960 to 1970, housing stock increased by 41 percent. But, between 1970 and 1976, it increased an additional 24 percent. Housing prices in the study area were rising more rapidly than incomes when compared to the Pierce County area as a whole.

The study found that the primary governmental function that was being provided to local citizens was education for children. The second and third deliverables were fire and police protection. To pay for these services, the county relied on funds from state and federal sources, along with money raised by the property tax. These sources accounted for about three-fourths of local revenue. Property taxes in the study area were considered below the statewide norm.

# A Community History

A home in the Manorwood neighborhood on South Hill, designed by Pete Naccarato and constructed by Heritage Homecrafters as part of the 1976 Tacoma Home Show. The 3,600-square-foot home featured five bedrooms, three bathrooms, cedar siding and a cedar shingle roof. This photograph was ordered by Homebuilders Association of Greater Tacoma. *Courtesy of Tacoma Public Library, Richards Studio Collection, D16670416.*

The study also considered the need to maintain open spaces as the population continued to increase. It was professed that open space should be classified as an economic public good. The authors observed that some of the benefits of open spaces included scenic beauty, environmental advantages and educational value to the public at large. The authors recommended that this could be accomplished by public purchase, restrictive zoning, public purchase of development rights, transfer of development rights and preferential assessments.

## Scientist, Activist, Environmentalist

One of the local citizens who arose to champion the cause of environmental conservation was Allen Zulauf, who has a long history of community involvement and activism on South Hill. As a soil scientist, Allen also has a great interest and concern for regional environmental issues.

His connection to soil started as a child, listening to his teacher Mrs. Brown talk about the Dust Bowl of the Great Depression and how tough life was in the 1930s. It made quite an impression on a kid who was growing up in the highly urbanized area of metropolitan New York and New Jersey. (Allen could see the Empire State building from his bedroom.) Allen said he always wanted to work in agriculture and save the soil. He admired the work of the Civilian Conservation Corps. He remembered that, during World War II, his mother worked the night shift, producing plastic for airplane canopies and gun turrets. There was a lot of pollution from the plant's emissions, making it difficult to breathe in the summer. The factory was only a mile from his house. His mother "was happy for having a job but came home with clothes reeking of organic chemicals."

In 1950, Allen was drafted into the Korean War, but rather than sail to Korea, as many of his friends did, he sailed to France. When he returned home, he and his brother developed a small package delivery business, serving metropolitan New York and upper New Jersey. Encouraged by his other brother, a University of Oregon graduate, he moved to Oregon and entered Portland State College. Allen became very attached to the Northwest because "it's the greatest part of the country to live in." He used the Korean War G.I. Bill to pay for his college expenses after graduating from Oregon State in 1954 with a degree in soils. The Soil Conservation Service in Washington State later employed him. He eventually transferred to Puyallup to complete the soil survey of Pierce County and led a state and federal group to provide watershed resource information to Puget Sound governments.

In 1968, Allen and his wife, Ellen, along with their three children, moved to South Hill. Their first house on the Hill was located on 107th Street, right off 86th Avenue. The backyard of the house bordered a raspberry field, where Allen pictured his kids picking berries in the summer. "Those thoughts were swept away with the field being in the path of 512," he stated.

Besides his professional career, Allen involved himself in the community. He took on traffic congestion. Strip malls were beginning to line Meridian Avenue, and it was "being choked" by cars, making it difficult to enter and leave these businesses. The South Hill Community Council focused on one development and pushed for access by side streets to and from the stores, with the streets connecting to intersections on Meridian Avenue.

In the 1960s and 1970s, land use plans on South Hill were not adequate. There was little effort by the county commissioners to do anything about it. In Allen's opinion, a very dramatic change for the better came with the formation of a charter government. The Pierce County Council replaced three men who made all the decisions that affected the county. Allen, a strong environmentalist, was the chair of the Puyallup River Watershed Council (earning the Citizen Watershed Steward Award in 2008) and former board member of Citizens for a Healthy Bay. Allen believes that the next generation of voters will be more sensitive to the environment than the current generation.

## "Pray for Me, I Drive Meridian"

In the 1970s, people on South Hill began to discuss problems with Meridian Avenue. After that, in addition to traffic congestion, local citizens started to complain about strip malls, comparing areas alongside Meridian Avenue to those at Sixth Avenue in Tacoma and South Tacoma Way. Unfortunately, neither state nor local governments had planned for this degree of expansion. Funds had not been allocated to make Meridian Avenue a reasonable thoroughfare. It was in 1978, for example, that the State Highway Department acknowledged that the traffic volume on Meridian Avenue was two and a half times its capacity. A widening was not in any plan for the next several years.

The road was officially named Meridian Avenue in 1983, when the county went to the present-day grid system. But in that grid system, it was also labeled as 102$^{nd}$ Avenue East, and in Washington State's official designation, it is State Route 161.

Meridian Avenue continued to be an overcrowded two-lane road throughout the 1980s and early 1990s. Some drivers even displayed bumper stickers that read, "Pray for me, I drive Meridian." At various times during that period, citizen groups tried to get the road improved. Some had a smidgen of success, such as the addition of turn lanes. In the late 1990s, this condition changed when the state legislative delegation from South Hill was successful in convincing state budget writers to fund the widening of Meridian Avenue.

During the development of the South Hill Community Plan in 2002 and 2003, an attempt was made to create alternatives around South Hill for those road users who lived to the south and used it just for commuting. Also, a scheme was debated to widen Meridian Avenue for a light rail line to provide commuter services. Both proposals failed to make the final design.

# South Hill, Washington

## Planning Sunrise

In 1983, a group of local developers, including Dick Crowe, launched a significant new planned community called the Rainier Terrace Master Planned Community, which was to be situated east of Thun Field and between 160th Street and 176th Street East—some 1,500 acres of total development. According to Crowe, it took fifteen years "to get the entitlements and legalities in line for construction. It was a pressure-packed deal because the Hill had no sewers (everything was septic), and 10,000 people were expected to live there."

Crowe saw hope to tap into sewer lines when Boeing purchased land in Frederickson, just west of South Hill, for an assembly plant. Boeing "brought in a twenty-four-inch pipe that linked to Chambers Creek Treatment Center," said Crowe. "I got a latecomer hookup for $6 million, but the county reneged."

Some local residents were vehemently opposed to the Rainier Terrace development. Although the "craziness of the housing boom sucked us all in," according to Crowe, there was significant opposition to the development. Dick noted that, at one meeting, a finger-pointing South Hill resident stood up and said, "You, sir, are killing the tall people! The tall people were the trees!"

Eventually, developer Terry Corliss, with Sunrise Development Corporation, bought out the project and took up where Crowe and his team left off. When homes finally went up in the late 1990s, the development carried the designation of Sunrise.

According to Crowe, "Sunrise was the answer to South Hill's sewers problem." Indeed, "Eventually, with all the new construction, that area of South Hill got sewers. Whatever was flushed one day arrived at Chambers Creek Treatment Center at Steilacoom two days later [after the plug-in with Frederickson]."

## Immigrant Family Benefits South Hill

### By Debbie Burtnett

In 1981, Erwin Kettner, who had settled in Puyallup decades earlier, phoned his cousin Helmut Rieder and Helmut's wife, Inge, in Germany and invited them to visit—and visit they did. They fished, hunted, boated and rode quarter horses in the mountains. After that, it took Erwin about a year to

## Building the South Hill Mall

*By Don De Salvo, General Partner,
Cafaro Northwest Partnership*

The development of the South Hill Mall started after I met with the Target people in the late 1980s, and we agreed to do a number of deals with them. With the market in Puyallup, I figured we'd get at least half a million feet on the ground, get there first and then grow. Once we came out of the ground with Target, everyone in the world was going to chase these guys. I had a good agreement with Target. With Target, we had Mervyn's because they owned Mervyn's. Mervyn's went in where the current J.C. Penney store is on the front of the mall, facing Meridian Avenue. We had Lamonts, too, which was a junior department store where Dick's is now. So, we had a decent little community shopping center.

But we knew the market was growing so fast that we needed more square footage, and the way that we do business in most of our middle-market facilities is that we build as much as we can with present-value dollars in mind and let the market grow with us, come to us, if we're in a growth arena. Our kind of philosophy is not to go in and be a small frog in a big pond. We want to be a big frog in a small pond and grow with the pond. We build as much as we can so that we can grow with the growth of the community we're in. We spent quite a bit of money on South Hill, and we continue to spend a lot of money to keep it fresh. We become a part of the fabric of the community, which we grow with our properties.

In the mid-1990s, we doubled the size of the mall. We went from 500,000 to over 1 million square feet. We mitigated everything. We widened Meridian Avenue, we widened the bridge across 512 and we widened 9$^{th}$ Street. We did that because we need people to get in and out as much as the city needs to get people to have a flow of traffic to get to and from places. We even sold close to an acre of our corner to Pierce Transit.

We continued to grow. When we dropped anchor in Puyallup, the population of the city was around 35,000, and the average household income was under $40,000. We stretched out and

An aerial view of the South Hill Mall in 2019. *Courtesy of Don De Salvo/ Cafaro Company.*

picked up 125,000 people in our market, which is good for a mall. Now, we're close to 350,000.

We don't like to go into a community that's not big enough to support what we're doing. And there has to be a growth component to it. We're involved with Pierce College, for example. We support Pierce College with grants. We do not build shopping centers that are not a part of the fabric. We want the continuum.

Puyallup is getting big, but it's not too big for what I'm talking about. It's a very connected and very determined community that doesn't want to grow out of its shoes. You go from growing hops to what we have now on the Hill, we have to take it into the next generation of commerce with things that will keep our kids in Puyallup.

convince Inge's family that she should move to America, "breaking a five-hundred-year-old tradition of running the family hostel." In 1982, the Rieders arrived in America on visas. They returned to Germany in 1986 but came back to the United States for good in 1990, and they set down roots on South Hill.

# A Community History

The sale of Helmut's businesses in Germany, including a large drycleaning enterprise, formed a large portion of the seed money for his ventures on South Hill. Helmut started Rieder Construction, whose Arabella development was on South Hill. Located at 139th Street East and Meridian Avenue, across from Firgrove School, Arabella was a twenty-unit ("duplex-houses") community that included the home in which he and Inge lived. As a developer and general contractor, Rieder incorporated European quality and design into his buildings at Arabella. Arabella's amenities included a gated entry, as well as brickwork, lighting, landscaping, a pond and waterfall and a private executive golf course.

The development was set back on Meridian Avenue when it was only a two-lane road with trees right up to the pavement. Since then, the space between the housing development and Meridian Avenue was developed into a business park in 1995. The business park included a medical building that was home to an orthopedic clinic, physical therapy clinic and foot and ankle clinic.

Helmut wanted to build another medical building and drove Meridian Avenue up and down to find just the right property—1803 South Meridian. The building has served as a physical therapy office and an urgent care

The Rieder Medical Building near Good Samaritan Hospital. *Courtesy of South Hill Historical Society.*

center, and it houses Mary Bridge facilities today. Following this success, two more medical buildings were located on the Good Samaritan campus. The first, Rieder Medical Building, houses women's specialists, a neurology group, internists, a family practice and a laboratory. The structure, totaling thirty thousand square feet, with parking, has served patients since 2006.

Florian Rieder, Helmut and Inge's son, supervised the construction of an eight-thousand-square-foot facility, which is now totally leased by Meridian Rehabilitation Center. The services offered in the European-style facility include physical therapy, chiropractic work, therapy treatments in a large pool and a smaller pool and massage therapy. The facility also has examination rooms, gym equipment and a spa. In 2008, the Rieders sold Arabella Business Park, but they maintain close contacts with the owners of the businesses and friends who live in the duplexes.

# 9
# PUBLIC PLACES AND SERVICES

Water has always been a problem on South Hill. The struggle is not to get rid of the rain that falls during most of the winter months but a need to have enough useable water to maintain a normal lifestyle. This may seem to be an irrelevant issue to most people who now live on the Hill; after all, you just turn on the faucet and the water flows. Historically, however, useable water was not always available in the neighborhood.

Early settlers on the Hill dug their own wells. At first, the digging was done by hand, but as time passed, it was done by drilling. After the Tacoma water reservoir was constructed, there were stories of local folks tapping into its wooden pipeline to obtain water. Several family histories of early settlers tell stories of traveling to water sources in wagons, filling fifty-gallon drums and bringing them back to the farm for family and cattle usage. So, the availability of useable water has always been a problem.

## THE FIRGROVE MUTUAL WATER COMPANY

Around the middle of the twentieth century, a group of about fifty farmers in the Firgrove area decided to try a more systematic approach to the water dilemma. They created a domestic farmstead water system. They initially started formulating this idea around 1945, and by 1952, they had created

Firgrove Mutual Water Company serves about ten square miles of South Hill. *Courtesy of South Hill Historical Society.*

a mutual water company. The idea of a mutual organization gave each member a part ownership and assured that each user would pay a fair share. They named the business the Firgrove Mutual Water Company.

When Firgrove Mutual was founded in 1952, it comprised forty-eight members. Its initial capital was $14,400, and it was estimated that $66,000 was needed to develop a source and construct a distribution system. A loan of $50,000 was obtained from the Federal Farm Home Administration, and land was purchased. The first building was constructed in 1953; it was a concrete block house and originally held two pressure tanks. It was converted to office use in the 1960s. In the 1980s, the current office was constructed on 144th Street East.

In 1982 a study by Pierce County, it was determined that, at that time, Firgrove Mutual had 1,317 connections and 12 sources of water. It had a storage capacity of 1,589,000 gallons. The company was successfully operated by its members and was growing as the Hill became more populated.

By 2001, after another twenty years, the number of Firgrove Mutual accounts had increased to 5,591, serving a population estimated at 17,500. That year, the company pumped 763,000,000 gallons of water. Mutual's annual report for 2010 showed there were 8,199 connections (or owners) in the system, serving a population of about 25,129. Water was obtained from 16 operating wells scattered throughout the service area. About 1.06 billion gallons of water were produced in 2010.

Firgrove Mutual provides useable water to an approximately ten-mile-square area of South Hill. It is an outstanding example of cooperative workmanship among the citizens of South Hill to solve a common problem.

## Fire Protection on the Hill

Organized fire protection on South Hill is a relatively new service. Central Pierce Fire & Rescue is now that provider (with some coverage from Graham Fire & Rescue in its area). But during the early periods of settlement on South Hill, there was no fire department. If there was a fire, neighbors either helped each other or just let it burn.

Until the mid-1940s, the population on the Hill was so low that supporting a fire department seemed impractical. But that thinking started to change as the number of inhabitants increased, and in 1947, a group of citizens was gathered to initiate the process of forming a basic volunteer fire department. Their plan did not include South Hill as we know it today, but it was a start, and they had a vision for expansion. About a year later, in April 1948, a proposal was submitted to the voters. It passed. Thus, 1948 is the year that firefighting gear was first bought, an engine was procured and a fire station was built. Voters approved $4 million to make this happen.

The first station was built at 114th Street and Canyon Road, and it was completed in January 1950. Its primary service areas were the communities of Summit, Woodland and Collins, and it was known as the Summit-Woodland-Collins Fire Department. In 1954, service was expanded to the Waller Road District, but it was not until 1958 (ten years after the department was formed) that South Hill proper was serviced, when coverage to the Willows and Firgrove communities was included. To support this expansion, the first fire station on the Hill was built at 116th Street and 94th Avenue. All of the department's personnel were volunteers until 1964, when the first paid firefighter was hired. Medical response services (EMS) were added in 1969.

The name of the group was changed in 1972 to the Summit Fire Department. Shortly afterward, in 1973, a new station was built on the Hill at 128th Street and 98th Avenue. It is still in use, as it replaced the older one, which was abandoned.

# South Hill, Washington

The Sunrisers Kiwanis Club presented its "Everyday Hero" Award to first responders from Central Pierce Fire and Rescue for saving a South Hill man's life. *Left to right*: Battalion Chief Baron Bannis, Paramedic Dan Osborne, Captain Mack Lycan, Becky Reece and Jerry Reece. *Courtesy of Sunrisers Kiwanis Collection.*

Still, in the early 1970s, the firefighting service was primarily a volunteer group. The first paid firefighters on the Hill were hired in 1976 and worked from the 128th Street facility. In 1978, the name was changed to the Summit-South Hill Fire Department. In 1986, an additional fire station was built on the eastern side of Thun Field, on 110th Avenue, next to what is now the Clover Park Technical College. It was not until 1998 that it was staffed full time. The current name for these firefighters was established in 1994. In that year, the Summit-South Hill group merged with the Parkland, Midland and Spanaway departments to become Central Pierce Fire & Rescue. And in 2002, the department finally became a totally professional agency; it no longer depends on volunteers.

## The Airports of South Hill

South Hill's airport is owned and operated by Pierce County and is officially known as the Pierce County Airport. It is best known as Thun Field. The airport was developed by John Thun during the 1950s and 1960s, but he

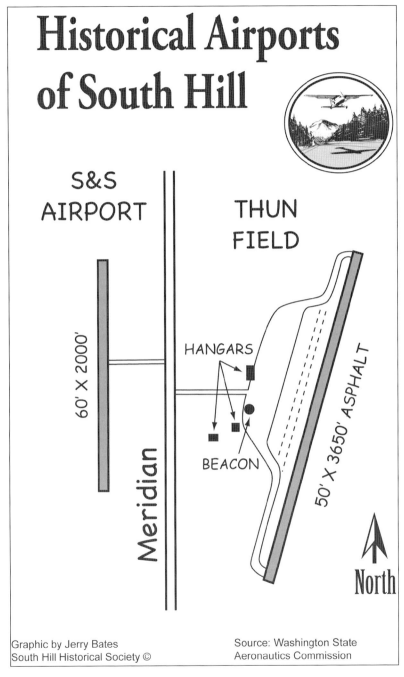

The airports of South Hill (pictured are Sagmiller and Thun Field). *Courtesy of Jerry Bates and the South Hill Historical Society.*

## South Hill, Washington

Lieutenant Don Angeline landed this P-51 Mustang fighter at South Hill's new airfield in 1946, before it was transported down Meridian Avenue and delivered to the Puyallup High School Aviation Program. *Courtesy of Pierce County Airport Collection.*

did not originate this landing field—nor was it the first aviation facility on South Hill.

James Sagmiller created the first airport on South Hill in the late 1930s. Before moving to the area, he had operated an aviation business in his home state of North Dakota, where he had been engaged in crop dusting and agricultural aviation–related activities. His intent was to move that enterprise to the farming areas of the Puyallup Valley. The airfield he built was located at the intersection of present-day Meridian Avenue East and 168th Street. A Walmart store and parking lot now occupy the site of that airstrip. While it was never prominent, this facility was listed in flying directories until the 1960s under the name S&S Airport.

In late 1944, a new airport was opened at a location directly across the road from the S&S Airport location, on the east side of Meridian Avenue. A group of Puyallup businessmen acquired the site and formed a company, not

*Right*: A promotional poster for the 1961 Thun Field Fly-in. *Courtesy of Pierce County Airport Collection.*

*Below*: John Thun. *Courtesy of Pierce County Airport Collection.*

## South Hill, Washington

to support agriculture but to provide a place for aviation training for returning war veterans. The attempt did not go well. There were still restrictions on private aircraft usage due of the war effort; moreover, the airstrip was never developed to acceptable standards. Eventually, it was essentially abandoned.

In 1949, Thun bought the discarded airport acreage. Thun was an aviation enthusiast, but he was not a pilot. He moved his family from their South Hill poultry farm (around present-day 144th Street East and 126th Avenue East) to the site and set about creating an acceptable airstrip. In this endeavor, he was successful, and over the next twenty years, he established a first-class airport with modern facilities. A number of local flyers used it for recreational purposes. There was some limited commercial activity, too, and on occasion, the military landed aircraft there when McChord Air Force Base was fogged in or overcrowded.

Thun sold the airport in 1967. A group of Puyallup businessmen—investors rather than airport operators—took control for a short period. They subsequently sold the business to an individual—again, an investor. It remained in his hands until the county bought the property in late 1979. The county paid just over $1 million for the installation, funded primarily

An air show at Thun Field in the early 1960s. The one-story airfield diner on the left side of the photograph adjoins the Thun family home. *Courtesy of Pierce County Airport Collection.*

(89 percent) by grants from the Federal Aviation Administration and the Washington State Department of Transportation. The airport remains a county facility to this day.

In 2006, Clover Park Technical College established a new aviation program on the edge of Thun Field, preparing local residents for careers in the aerospace and aviation fields.

## Rogers High School

In 1966, Puyallup High School was so overcrowded that double sessions were considered. That year, the school board approved a plan to build a second high school in the district. Puyallup High School vice principal Art Larson, a navy veteran of World War II and the Korean conflict, was selected to be the principal of the new school. Art was tasked with planning an entire institution, with a new curriculum to be designed, new district lines to be drawn and new teachers to recruit and hire. Today, most new principals would take a year off their regular duties for all the necessary planning, but back then, Art was expected to carry on his vice principal duties as usual along with the huge workload for the new school. It was a daunting task.

For example, consider the logistics. Some kids would not be graduating from the school they and their parents had planned on. Many parents were upset about breaking a family tradition. Some had four generations who graduated from Puyallup High School. Art spent long hours with families from South Hill, working to convince them that it was worthwhile for their student to attend the new high school. "We kind of horned in on the PTA meetings at the elementary schools," he recalled. "It was up to me to convince people that it wasn't all bad." Some of the parents with whom Art spoke had been his students at Puyallup High School years earlier, and he quickly won them over.

When it came to selecting a name for the new school, school board member Vitt Ferrucci proposed the name of Governor John R. Rogers, a longtime populist writer and activist who settled in Puyallup in the late 1800s, served in the legislature and served as Washington's third governor. It turned out that Ferrucci's wife had graduated from Spokane's high school by that name. "He thought that we needed something on this side," said Art. Ferrucci won over his fellow board members, and they selected Rogers for the school's name.

# South Hill, Washington

When it came time to choose the school colors, a mascot and a title for the school newspaper and yearbook, a community committee was formed to make the decisions. The ram was chosen as the mascot. It was Art who proposed and won approval for the school colors: navy blue, inspired by Art's navy service; and Columbia blue, inspired by his time at navy midshipman school at Columbia University.

Art and his team also designed a new curriculum for Rogers High School. It included multiple tracks for college-bound students and those pursuing vocational careers. This curriculum was called the "comprehensive high school"—offering academics, remedial instruction and vocational education, usually in one or more of the sciences—an innovation in education during the 1960s. Art had sympathy for the kids who had a hard time in their academic classes. He wanted a school that wasn't just for athletes and the "intelligentsia." They created shop classes, auto shop, metal shop, woodshop, mechanical drawing, home economics classes, agricultural classes and even classes on how to be waiters, waitresses and cooks. "The goal was to offer a wide variety of subjects that kids were interested in and match with his or her talents and skills," he said. Art was aware of the students who loved art, so the school had classes in sculpture, painting and theater. He was a principal ahead of his time. Arrangements were made to bus students between the old and new campuses to share facilities and offer classes that were not available at one of the home campuses to all of the area's students.

Sue Croy of the class of 1971, Rogers High School's first Daffodil Princess. *Courtesy of the Rogers High School yearbook, Walt Zeiger Collection.*

Moving day for the partially completed Rogers High School was in the fall of 1968. The classrooms were full of hanging wires and workmen. The cafeteria and gym were yet to be completed. The first year started with seventh through tenth grades. The second year, Rogers offered seventh to eleventh grades. When Ballou Junior High was finished, Rogers offered tenth through twelfth grade, with the class of 1971 as the first graduating class. Some of the early students attended Rogers for five years.

Art was very proud of the quality of teachers at the school. He described his position as principal as "very fortunate," as he had really great teachers in all departments.

*Left*: The program cover for one of the first Rogers versus Puyallup football games, October 2, 1970. *Courtesy of Walt Zeiger.*

*Below*: Art Larson guided the creation of South Hill's first high school named after John R. Rogers, Washington States' third governor. *Courtesy of South Hill Historical Society.*

He considered his math department one of the best. Such excellent faculty, no doubt, was due to Art's hiring philosophy. "Just being smart didn't make a good teacher; a teacher had to be highly competent in the field [he or she] would teach," and Art looked for good disciplinarians—the ability to get along with students yet control a classroom.

Art was the principal at Rogers High School for eleven years before retiring in 1979, still in his fifties. Art had no trouble filling the following years with activity, as he was an active member of the Puyallup Rotary Club, a teaching instructor at PLU and a worker at the Puyallup Fair. Paul Hackett has summed up Art's life best when he said, "Speaking as a former pastor, Art has been a shepherd to the whole community, not just as the high school principal, but in working and caring for others and in making life meaningful."

## First Legal Garbage Dump on South Hill

Getting rid of garbage is a problem that is common to all societies. South Hill has not been an exception. Burying it, burning it or dumping it in some river can all be considered possible solutions. Like in most rural areas, however, the first settlers on the Hill did not really see this as a problem. There was plenty of open space, burning could be done easily and livestock could consume the leftovers. But as the population increased and the size of farms and open spaces decreased, the disposal of waste did become an issue.

It cannot be exactly pinpointed when formalized garbage collection started on the Hill. We do know that such services were being provided by the mid-twentieth century. In 1953, a study by the Tacoma-Pierce County Health Department, for example, listed ten companies that were licensed to haul garbage in Pierce County. South Hill was being serviced by the Pierce County Refuse Company, which was owned by Harold E. LeMay. The collected waste was being hauled to the Tacoma City Dump.

By the early 1950s, the trash on South Hill was being both collected and properly buried in a licensed landfill, but it was recognized that these practices could not be continued. The travel distances involved and the cost of transporting an ever-growing amount of garbage called for a waste disposal site closer to the sources of pickup. It was this thinking that motivated the county commissioners to purchase about twenty acres of real estate on South Hill for the purpose of establishing a local landfill site in July 1953. The site was located in Section 20 of Township 19, identified today as the northeast corner at the intersection of Woodland Avenue and 160th Street. This land was in the so-called Starvation Valley area of South Hill, so the dump was officially named the Starvation Valley Garbage Dump. The county bought the land from the West Tacoma Newsprint Company for $175. Another $46,926 was spent developing it for use.

This waste disposal site was originally a shallow-fill design. There were no provisions for burning. But by the 1960s, local residents noticed deep ditches being dug and witnessed the start of incineration. In 1966, citizens initiated a petition to stop any expansion. As a result, county officials assured the residents that the landfill site would be used for only a few more years and that a new location farther away from residential growth would be developed. In 1968, the county was forced by citizen complaints to again take action—this time, to prevent the site from also being used as a shooting range.

The Starvation Valley Garbage Dump was gradually being closed by the end of the 1960s. Starting as early as 1967, refuse was being taken to a site at Thun Field, an old gravel pit located just off the south end of the airport runway.

## Hidden Valley Landfill

South Hill's modern landfill, like its predecessor, has not been without controversy and environmental challenges. Over the years, it has been considered one of the most polluted spots in Pierce County. It has received attention from three levels of environmental agencies: federal, state and local. Located near the southeast intersection of Meridian Avenue and 176th Street, the spot is known as the Hidden Valley Landfill, or the Pierce County Landfill. The location is important because it overlies the Central Pierce County Aquifer System, a sole-source water pool for a large number of citizens on South Hill.

The Federal Environmental Protection Agency (EPA) has designated this place a superfund site. Superfund is the shorthand name for the Federal Comprehensive Environmental Response, Compensation and Liability Act of 1980. This designation gives federal authorities the right to identify and to clean up hazardous substances that may endanger human health or the environment.

The problem was created some five decades ago. In 1967, for example, the ninety-two-acre setting was operating both as a gravel pit and as a landfill.

According to the EPA, until 1985, the landfill accepted liquids, solids, industrial wastes and heavy metal sludges. Most importantly, it was determined that fifty-six acres under the landfill had no ground protection. During its investigation, the EPA declared that the "groundwater beneath the site and leachate in the landfill are contaminated with metals, volatile organic compounds (VOCs), and nitrates." And since there was no liner, it was anticipated that rainwater would filter through the collection, and eventually, all the contaminants could be deposited into South Hill's only water source.

The EPA proposed placing the site on its National Priorities List (NPL) in 1986. The listing was accomplished in 1989. It was also in 1989 that the unprotected landfill stopped accepting waste and clean up began. One early action was the installation of a gas control system. This effort has been modified several times during the past two decades; most recently, it was modified to convert waste into energy and supply electricity to a compost facility adjacent to the landfill.

In 1992, a Remedial Investigation and Feasibility Study of the location was completed. In 2000, a final Cleanup Action Plan (CAP) was finished. The required remedial action was aimed at minimizing production and movement of water through the fill. According to EPA records, the required corrective actions included covering the waste with an impermeable barrier to keep water from leaking into the ground; collecting landfill gases; controlling surface water and soil erosion; limiting human and animal contact with the waste; and minimizing the lateral and vertical movement of contaminated groundwater. CAP ultimately required that the landfill be closed, which was done. An additional requirement was that the site was to be monitored for compliance, and approved institutional controls were implemented. As of 2010, the site was still on EPA's National Priorities List.

While most of the site remains closed, Hidden Valley Landfill continues to provide garbage, recycling and yard waste disposal services for thousands of local residents.

## The South Hill Library

The South Hill library, a branch of the Pierce County Library System, is a very busy place. In fact, it is one of the most extensively used branches of the system. In 2011, some thirty-four thousand people used the facility, checking out over one million items. To use one of the sixty-two computer stations, you have to sign in and literally stand in line. Before the establishment of a library, local South Hill citizens had a variety of ways to get library services. Those fortunate enough to work for one of the various schools used the schools' collections whenever possible. But by far, the most commonly used library was the one located in Puyallup. To the early South Hill residents, the Puyallup library, at 324 South Meridian Avenue, was the most accessible, well-established and friendly library in the area. While it was independently owned by the city, it also served county residents.

The Pierce County independent Rural Library District was not established until 1946, even though Pierce County had been in existence for over a century. When the system was started, some library locations were selected, but the initial library planners did not include South Hill for a specific branch. It was not until 1968 that the county published a plan to develop new library locations. In that work, recommendations were made for expansion through 1985. The report suggested new facilities in the Lakes District, Gig Harbor and the Lower Peninsula. Again, South Hill was not included.

A bookmobile system provided limited library services to South Hill during the early days of district operations. By 1981, for example, South Hill had two scheduled routes: one operated on the first and third Thursdays of the month, while the second ran on the second and fourth Saturdays of the month. In combination, these mobile libraries stopped at eleven locations on the Hill. The stops included both commercial and residential areas and connected many people to the library system.

South Hill Library, from bookmobile to one of the most extensively used branches of the Pierce County Library System. *Courtesy of South Hill Historical Society.*

The first public library facility opened on South Hill in November 1982. While it was a lending library, it was not a dedicated standalone facility. Rather, the operation was a store-front venture located at 12020 Meridian Avenue, Suite E, in the Plaza II Shopping Center. It was a small area of 3,237 square feet, was only open for twenty-seven hours a week and had the equivalent of two employees. Today, that space is occupied by the L.A. Tanning salon.

The library that we know today was opened in 1990. It was the result of a county bond issue in 1986. When construction was completed, it replaced the store-front undertaking that had then been in place for eight years. In 2006, voters again approved a levy to improve the branch.

## Pierce College Puyallup

*Top*: Earl Hale, the executive director of the state's community college system, speaks at the opening of Pierce College's Puyallup Campus in 1990 as Pierce College president Frank "Buster" Brouillet and Governor Booth Gardner sit behind him. *Courtesy of Pierce College Collection.*

*Bottom*: The construction of the Pierce College Puyallup Campus in the late 1980s. *Courtesy of Pierce College Collection.*

# A Community History

## Bradley Lake Park

Bradley Lake, today's centerpiece of a marvelous city of Puyallup park, was named after the land's former owner, Ward Bradley, who acquired it in 1955. Ward Bradley was born on October 9, 1918, in Jamestown, North Dakota. He grew up on a farm. In 1938, he enlisted in the navy. He left the military in 1945, after having served in both the Atlantic and Pacific theaters during World War II. In the 1950s, Bradley won a federal civil service appointment as a postal mail carrier on South Hill. On his route was a farm that was owned by M.J. Combs, located at the eastern end of what was then 104$^{th}$ Street East. After some discussion, Mr. Combs agreed to swap this farm for some property that Bradley owned in the Columbia Basin. At the time, 104$^{th}$ Street was a gravel road off Meridian Avenue. There were no buildings on either side of the road between the farmhouse and Meridian Avenue. The closest neighbor was Louis Barth, who was located on a hill to the west. On the south side was the property of Dr. McKay, who had a medical practice in his home.

When Bradley acquired the property, a peat bog was located at the site of today's lake. Since there was a market for dried peat, he gradually

Cows graze near Ward Bradley's lake in the 1970s. *Courtesy of Don Massie.*

## South Hill, Washington

Once a peat bog, Bradley Lake Park on South Hill is the pride of the Puyallup Park System. *Courtesy of South Hill Historical Society.*

began a mining effort to remove it. He did this as a part-time pursuit with the help of some hired labor. It was mostly done during the summer so that the peat could be stacked to dry for sale during the winter. For over thirty years, Bradley systematically removed peat from the bog. He started on the north end and worked toward the south. However, he never completely finished, and in 1980, he hired a contractor to remove the rest. The company worked for approximately two months, using a track-powered dragline bucket. For drying, the peat was stockpiled around the farmhouse and in other buildings. In total, Bradley estimated that 300,000 to 400,000 yards of peat were removed. During that period, peat sold between $2.50 and $5.00 per cubic yard, delivered.

After the peat was removed, Bradley built a dam on the north end of the former bog. It took about six thousand yards of earth to create this barrier. A clay core was placed in the wall, along with a concrete spillway. Rain soon filled the hole, and Bradley Lake was formed. The maximum depth in the southern two-thirds of the pond is about twenty feet, with eight to twelve feet being the maximum on the north end.

The city first attempted to purchase the property in 1994. A bond issue was proposed but was turned down by the voters. In 1997, the project was reconsidered and again placed on the ballot. The voters approved the acquisition in 1998. Since then, the city has created a park that is enjoyed by all.

## South Hill Community Park

Decades of effort went into the development of the South Hill Community Park. Thanks to the faith and determination of Sherri Bails, South Hill has a park that all enjoy today. "The Park at 144th and 84th [Streets] should be named Sherri Bails Park; it was a result of twenty years of her perseverance, with many saying it couldn't be done," said Pat Drake, a longtime **South Hill** resident and teacher.

The story begins in 1978, when four South Hill residents—**Larry Finnestad, Sherri Bails, LuAnne Foxford and Janelle Hooper**—formed SHORE (South Hill Outdoor Recreation and Education.) Its purpose was to acquire and develop park sites on South Hill. The organization approached Ward Bradley about purchasing his fifty scenic acres that had a lake and old barn for a park. The SHORE group got busy getting advice from the man who developed Snake Lake Park in Tacoma while Sherri wrote a prospectus. They got commitments from six school districts that were interested in bringing children to the site. For political help, the group gave state legislators George Walk, Marc Gaspard and Dan Grimm a tour of the site. Sherri said, "[The legislators] fell in love with the property and felt our enthusiasm."

The SHORE group set about trying to get state approval for a purchase agreement to develop the Bradley property. The legislators were able to secure $725,000 in state funds, but things fell apart when Bradley refused the state's offer. After all their hard work, they were back to square one. Then, "Dan Grimm had an idea!" said Sherri. His plan was a land swap with the State Department of Natural Resources to acquire a forty-acre parcel that was formerly used as a cow pasture on the corner of 144th Street East and 86th Avenue East, just south of Rogers High School. Because they had done so much work on the Bradley property, it was decided they could fold over all that effort and apply it to the new site. One problem remained— they needed $600,000 to finish the land swap. It was 1981, and there was a recession. Senator Marc Gaspard warned Sherri that her prospects were grim for getting the money from the capital budget. After many hours of debate—at the last moment with a line item, up or down vote—they got the one Republican vote they needed.

With the land swap completed, the county agreed to establish a park; SHORE was to be the catalyst for all the community groups that would help develop it. "We contacted every community group in Puyallup and South Hill to sign on and help, along with the legislators and interested individuals," said Sherri.

The group had the park property and knew how they wanted to develop it; however, they needed an unclassified use permit. Then, a long-running difference of visions for the park began between then–county parks director Jan Walcott and Sherri. The parks director, a former coach, imagined a park comprising ball fields. Sherri's vision was to preserve of woods and wetlands. Sherri and her group wanted to keep the old second-growth wooded area as a natural area of the park.

The group's struggle continued without funding, but that didn't stop them. They found voluntary help from the Boy Scouts and free dredging and grading from the national guard and a local contractor. "We were looking for money to develop this site, [but during] all those years, we used free labor to get it done without the help of anybody," said Sherri.

During the early 1990s, things finally turned around. State senator Calvin Goings secured $500,000 in state funding. Pierce County executive Doug Sutherland kept his promise to support the park. The county agreed to contribute $250,000. Sherri, with help from Pat Drake and others, obtained an additional grant of $241,000 from Microsoft billionaire Paul Allen, and their financing goals were met. Their years of effort were

The Nathan Chapman Trail begins in a wooded area of South Hill Park. *Courtesy of South Hill Historical Society.*

# A Community History

The Chapman Trail links South Hill Community Park with the Heritage Recreation Center. *Courtesy of South Hill Historical Society.*

finally realized—the park would be a reality. Shovels were ready and guests gathered for the April 1, 2000, groundbreaking. Sherri summed up the long years of struggle, saying, "I was never alone; basically, I kept it going. I put my finger in the dike and stubbornly kept it there." She also credited many "amazing occurrences" that happened during the long journey to her strong Christian faith. She was especially motivated by the Bible passage that says, "I will overcome the world."

In 2005, the portion of the South Hill Park trails that connects South Hill Park with the Heritage Park & Recreation Center was dedicated to the memory of SFC Nathan Chapman, the first American soldier killed in the Afghanistan War in January 2002. He was a member of the First Special Forces Group (Airborne) and a young husband and father. The family lived on South Hill.

## South Hill tries for cityhood

During the 1990s, citizens attempted to incorporate South Hill as a city. The name of the proposed municipality was Southview. According to a "Notice of Intention and Feasibility Study" that was submitted in June 1998 to the Pierce County Boundary Review Board, the proposal to create a city had its roots in citizen dissatisfaction with county government, particularly the perceived lack of attention the area was getting. This dissatisfaction had been building over a number of years and can actually be found referenced in media reports as early as the 1970s.

It all started coming to a head in the early to mid-1990s. Local citizen activists formed groups to address what they considered county management shortcomings. One of the first groups to take shape was the South Hill-Summit View Community Council. Its stated purpose was to bring together "local residents, business leaders and civic leaders to address some of the needs of the community." Early on, this group declared the need for citizens to have a greater say and more participation in local planning and land use issues. They requested that the county form a land use advisory board and community zoning plan. Both requests were rejected. So, with the lack of support and interest from Pierce County, the community council began exploring other options.

A second working group of interested citizens, including State Senator Calvin Goings, Carl Vest, Christine Wilson, Jim Tesso and Lori and William J. VanderPas, formed around the idea of incorporating a city. They called themselves the Cityhood for Southview Committee. Through the efforts of this group, a petition drive for incorporation was initiated. Completed petitions, which were signed by 10 percent of the registered voters residing within the limits of the proposed city, were filed with the county auditor on May 6, 1998. The auditor certified the sufficiency of the incorporation petition on June 1, 1998. By that time, the committee had also gained the support of a large number of local organizations.

As required by law, the proposal was submitted to the Pierce County Boundary Review Board for examination in August 1998. The board recommended against incorporation. Moreover, opposition surfaced from other sources, primarily land developers and others who generally lived outside the proposed city area but nevertheless had vested interests in keeping the area unincorporated and free from what they anticipated would be restricted development regulations. The proposed incorporation was submitted to the voters in November 1998. It was soundly defeated at the polls. Thus ended the Hill's only attempt to incorporate as a city.

# 10
# SOUTH HILL IN THE TWENTY-FIRST CENTURY

## The South Hill Community Plan

In the early 2000s, a volunteer group of South Hill citizens worked very hard to put together a plan for regulating development on the Hill. The design, which cost about $300,000, was passed into law by the Pierce County Council in 2003. It was titled the South Hill Community Plan and is still the controlling regulation for development in this part of Pierce County. It took almost four years to write the strategy. There were many public sessions in which the entire community was asked to contribute ideas and assist volunteers in producing an approach that would satisfy the needs of all future residents.

Why did South Hill need a plan to regulate development? The roots of this go back into the 1980s, when the Hill was experiencing uncontrolled growth. Throughout the state, at that time, the situation on Pierce County's South Hill was being used as a poster child of what not to do. During that period, many local communities were also starting to engage in formal growth planning processes, and they were justifying it by saying that they did not want to end up like South Hill. The pressure increased further after the state passed the Growth Management Act in 1990. To comply with the requirements in that law, Pierce County then decided to delegate to some communities the authority to work out designs for their local neighborhoods. The thought was that all the results could then be integrated into a master blueprint for the entire county.

## A Community History

The development of local community plans was delegated to volunteer citizen groups, which were appointed by the county council and supported by the county's Planning and Land Use (PALS) organization. The South Hill panel consisted of fifteen people, drawn from all parts of the community.

When the county adopted the South Hill ideas, there was, for the first time, a regulation in force that established zoning and land usage in a rational way. Development standards regarding curbing, sidewalks, lighting, signage, control of storm water and the like became a part of the overall requirements for developing both commercial and residential projects. Historic preservation was also recognized and authorized to stop the destruction of heritage places and buildings.

Finally, when looking at long-range requirements, two important citizen oversight bodies were created. First, to ensure that any future land use proposals fit into the established scheme, a South Hill Land Use Advisory Committee was established. Commonly known as SHAC (South Hill Advisory Committee), this group still exists and meets regularly to review proposed developments. The second authorization set up a Thun Field Advisory Committee. The airport was considered to be of such importance to South Hill that there should be close coordination between the people who use it and the community in general. This board is also still in place and meets quarterly. Both of these groups are staffed with local citizen volunteers.

Mount Rainier looms over an airplane parked at Thun Field. *Courtesy of Pierce County Archive.*

## Meridian Habitat Park

Ever since Betsy Stubbs moved to South Hill in 1981, she has kept a close eye on South Hill planning efforts by Pierce County government and developers. She is—or has been—a member of a long list of South Hill organizations and efforts to protect the livability of the Hill.

In the late 1980s, Betsy, along with others, formed South Hill Action to Protect the Environment. "We wanted to make sure there were public places to play, be outside and enjoy the beauty that makes up this state and the Hill," said Betsy. Betsy "eyed" the church property located at 144th Street and Meridian Avenue, seeing it as a great site for a future park. It was then owned by the Champions Centre Church and used for their annual *Jesus of Nazareth* production. She felt that "if that property ever came up for sale, the county [needed] to buy it." Betsy and the South Hill Community Council developed a document that listed a series of amenities that would enhance life on South Hill, one of which addressed the church property. Working with the South Hill Community Planning Board, the goal of acquiring the church property for a park became official. It was included in the South Hill Community Plan, which was adopted by the Pierce County Council in 2003 to manage development on South Hill.

In 2006, the church property became available on the real estate market, and the county bought it. Now that they had a park site, Betsy and the South Hill Community Council wanted to give the new Meridian Habitat Park a new "personality." "In my mind, that property had an identity crisis," said Betsy. "For many—having lived for any time on the Hill—it was still the place of the *Jesus of Nazareth* production." With the park's "personality goal" in mind, Betsy and her fellow South Hill Community Council members decided to hold the South Hill Tree Lighting Christmas event at Habitat Park. The event had been held annually for seven years at another location, and it continued in its new location at the park for the next ten years. "We had three elementary schools involved at one time, and teachers liked it; they could come say the word Christmas and sing Christmas songs and not worry about being politically correct." The South Hill Community Council Tree Lighting Event had essential support and help from Pierce County Parks & Recreation, the fire department and the sheriff's office. "The kids would each bring an ornament for local charity groups; it became a "real community thing," said Betsy. Sadly, over time, such a big project became more than the willing volunteers could support, and the last event was held in 2016.

# A Community History

*Left to right*: Betsy Stubbs, Sherri Bails (*seated*), Paul Silvernail, Carol Silvernail and Christine Wilson at the 2009 South Hill tree lighting at Meridian Habitat Park. *Courtesy of Betsy Stubbs.*

Since the park's identity was still an issue, Betsy and the South Hill Community Council decided South Hill Habitat Park needed a playground to attract park visitors. Betsy, who works with disabled children for the Puyallup School District, knew there was a need on the Hill for a place that disabled children could go to—a place where children with autism or those in wheelchairs, walkers and braces could play and have fun outdoors. A June 2010 *Puyallup Herald* article titled "South Hill Wants Place for All Kids to Play" featured Betsy's and the South Hill Community Council's vision for a "sensory" playground for kids with disabilities. The idea gained momentum. "Even Senator Patty Murray loved it; she came out and we walked her around," said Betsy. Six months later, the economy went downhill. The playground idea was considered pork-barrel spending and was put on the shelf.

Betsy and her park advocate friend Sherri Bails, didn't give up on the playground idea, and "finally, things started to happen." The county put a new playground plan forward. This time, it was to be done in phases—and construction got underway. A grand opening was held in the fall of 2016. Betsy maintains contact with the playground designers and builders, making sure their plans are conforming to a woodland theme, that it is safe and that meets the needs of all children.

*Above*: The nature-themed sensory playground at Meridian Habitat Park was opened in 2016. *Courtesy of Jerry Bates*.

*Left*: The Sway artwork adorns the entrances to Meridian Habitat Park. *Courtesy of South Hill Historical Society*.

A Community History

## South Hill Today

Two major new South Hill institutions opened their doors at the turn of the century. The YMCA inaugurated a large multipurpose activity center on 43$^{rd}$ Avenue Southeast in 2000, which was generously supported by longtime Puyallup car dealer Jerry Korum and named in honor of his father, Mel Korum. And the Puyallup School District opened its newest high school, Emerald Ridge, on the edge of the Sunrise development. Among the first students at Emerald Ridge was a swimmer named Megan Quann. Quann became internationally famous when she won two gold medals in the 2000 Summer Olympics in Sydney, Australia, at the age of sixteen. Today, a county road sign that welcomes people to South Hill proclaims it is the home of gold medalist Megan Quann.

South Hill has continued its long-running pattern of growth. South Hill now has a large, modern post office at 132$^{nd}$ Street and Meridian Avenue, and the Pierce County Sheriff's Department has its South Hill Precinct at 160$^{th}$ Street and Meridian Avenue. Hundreds of retail outlets have proliferated up and down Meridian Avenue. The Hill is host to two Walmart stores, two Target stores, two Ram restaurants, two Red Robin restaurants, two Applebees restaurants, three McDonald's restaurants, three Vietnamese pho restaurants and seven Starbucks coffee shops. The South Hill Mall, owned by the Ohio-based Cafaro Company, has remained an economic hub for the region for over thirty years, with 1.1 million square feet of retail space anchored by Target, Macy's, J.C. Penney, Dick's Sporting Goods, Regal Cinema, H&M and Designer Shoe Warehouse. Meanwhile, large new retail centers have opened along the Meridian Avenue corridor, including Tarragon Property Services' 550,000-square-foot Sunrise Village, which opened in 2008, with Target, LA Fitness, HomeGoods and PetSmart as its anchor venues.

The Hill is fertile ground for a number of houses of worship. Among the largest congregations are Motion Church at 160$^{th}$ Street and Meridian Avenue, Lighthouse Christian Center beside Highway 512 and Bethany Baptist Church near the mall. South Hill is also home to active congregations of the Church of Jesus Christ of Latter-Day Saints, including a stake center on 94$^{th}$ Avenue that hosts an annual ecumenical community Christmas concert.

The passage of a school bond in 2004 led to the construction of Emma Carson Elementary, George Edgerton Elementary and Glacier View Junior High School. Another bond in 2015 resulted in reconstructions

# South Hill, Washington

# A Community History

*Opposite, top*: Emerald Ridge is South Hill's newest high school. *Courtesy of South Hill Historical Society.*

*Opposite, bottom*: The Mel Korum Family YMCA, a multipurpose activity center, was opened in 2000 and remains a busy place on South Hill. *Courtesy of South Hill Historical Society.*

*Above*: At age sixteen, Megan Quann of South Hill won two gold medals in swimming at the 2000 Olympic Games in Sydney, Australia. Quann went on to graduate from Emerald Ridge High School in 2002. *Courtesy of McCutcheon Studio Collection.*

Members of the South Hill Sunrisers Kiwanis Club visited local schools to take part in Terrific Kid Assemblies. *Courtesy of Sunrisers Kiwanis Collection.*

of Firgrove Elementary and Sunrise Elementary and a remodel and expansion of Pope Elementary.

Even as more and more students go to school on the Hill, a growing population at the other end of the age spectrum is seeking living options on the Hill. A number of new senior residential facilities have opened on the Hill, with plans for more as of this writing.

In the fall of 2020, the Pierce County Council approved changes to the South Hill Community Plan, designating Longston Towne Center (along Meridian Avenue, between $126^{th}$ Street and $136^{th}$ Street) and Sunrise Village Towne Center (along Meridian Avenue, between $152^{nd}$ Street and $162^{nd}$ Street) as central gathering places for shopping, amenities and higher-density housing, such as apartments and townhouses.

Twenty years into a new millennium, South Hill continues to grow. According to Pierce County, the 2019 population of South Hill was 59,700 people—up from 35,500 at the turn of the millennium. Increasingly diverse families come here and put down roots, take part in local schools, enjoy South Hill's parks and recreation opportunities and attend local houses of worship. Residents work for local and regional employers, commute up and down South Hill's crowded corridors and catch majestic glimpses of

# A Community History

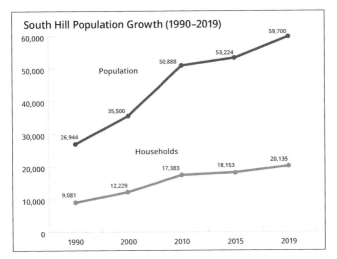

*Pierce County Planning and Public Works, 2020.*

Mount Rainier from time to time. South Hill is a largely unincorporated community of neighborhoods, a network of neighbors who share more in common than we may realize. Not least among the things we share is a rich history on our beloved Hill. Each of us can do our part to shape history as it unfolds into the future.

# SOUTH HILL HISTORY: A TIMELINE

**Pre-1870s**  Puyallup tribal members train young men and hunt on the Hill.

1853  The Longmire-Biles wagon train crosses South Hill.

1862  The Homestead Act of 1862 initiates a new era of western settlement.

1872  William Rankin Ballard surveys the Hill.

1870s  Carl Muehler, George and Theresa Mosolf and Alois Kupfer settle on South Hill.

1884  The Woodland School is established on land that was once owned by Ezra Meeker.

1889  Pierce County commissioners approve a petition for a new road on South Hill, with survey work funded by Harvey Ball and George Wood, earning the designation Ball-Wood Road (later renamed Meridian Avenue).
Washington Territory becomes a state.
The Tacoma Railway and Power Company Old Line Trolley begins service from Puyallup to Tacoma.

1895  The original Firgrove School is built.

## South Hill History: A Timeline

**1910**      The Forest Grove School District established (later renamed Puyallup Heights School).

**1920**      The construction of Shaw Road is completed.

**1930s**      Rabbit Farms is advertised as a destination with economic potential during the Great Depression.
Mitchell Gould Road (today's 152nd Street) is completed.

**1931**      The pavement of Puyallup-Graham Road (later renamed Meridian Avenue) is completed.

**1932**      Fruitland Grange is organized.

**1934**      The Woodland Bus Company is established, connecting the Hill to surrounding communities.

**1935**      A new brick Firgrove School building opens its doors to students.

**1939**      Al Delano buys most of the land around 112th Street and Meridian Avenue and establishes several businesses at what becomes known as Willows Corner.

**1944**      A business group starts a new airport venture near 160th Street and Meridian Avenue.

**1945**      Two Japanese balloon bombs land on South Hill.

**1948**      Voters approve the first fire station serving South Hill.
Highlands Community Church is established (today's Living Hope Church).

**1949**      John Thun buys the airfield near 160th Street and Meridian Avenue.

**1952**      The Firgrove Mutual Water Company is formed.

**1960**      Puyallup Dragway begins its first year of car races next to Thun Field.

# South Hill History: A Timeline

**1968**     John R. Rogers High School opens.

**1969**     South Hill citizens form T19A to push for better county planning.

**1972**     State Route 512 is completed as a four-lane highway.
The South Hill Community Development Organization continues the planning work that was started by T19A.

**1973**     The Willows Shopping Center opens at 112th Street and Meridian Avenue.

**1982**     The first public library facility opens on South Hill.

**1988**     The South Hill Mall opens.

**1990**     The South Hill Library moves into new building.

**1998**     City of Puyallup voters approve the acquisition of Bradley Lake as a new city park.
South Hill citizens attempt to incorporate Southview as a city, but the measure fails at the ballot.

**2000**     The Mel Korum Family YMCA opens.
Emerald Ridge High School opens.

**2001**     The South Hill Historical Society is founded.

**2002**     South Hill's Megan Quann wins two gold medals in swimming at the Olympic Games in Sydney, Australia.

**2005**     Nathan Chapman Trail is dedicated, connecting South Hill Park with Heritage Park and Recreation Center.

**2006**     Pierce County purchases the former church property at 144th Street and Meridian Avenue for use as a park and community center known as Meridian Habitat Park.

# ACKNOWLEDGEMENTS

This book exists because of Carl Vest's tireless effort to write South Hill's history over the past two decades. It is also possible because of Paul Hackett's ambitious campaign to interview longtime South Hill citizens, starting in 2001. And we owe thanks to those who have contributed writings to the South Hill Historical Society Newsletter over the years. Through the newsletter, which Jerry Bates has edited for most of its existence, the society has amassed a large collection of primary writings and other historical accounts. And there are those who have built the society and kept it going since 2001. Ben Peters was among the society's cofounders, along with Carl Vest and Paul Hackett. The presidents of the society have included Don Glaser, Bob Ballou, Wes Perkinson and Yvonne Thorpe. Along with Carl Vest, the following members or friends of the society contributed portions of this book:

Jerry Bates
Beverly Olin Brunet
Debbie Burtnett
Don De Salvo
Bill Goelzer
Paul Hackett
Barbara Huff Ringo
Helen Heil Rohlman
Joan Parks Vosler

## Acknowledgements

Among those who aided with the search for historic South Hill photographs were Patricia Drake; Pierce County councilmember Dave Morell; Judy Hurley and Kyle Schmidtke of Pierce County; Lissa Smith of Thun Field; Brian Benedetti of Pierce College; Don De Salvo and David Montevideo of the Cafaro Company; Gail Ostheller of Living Hope Church; Ron Pearson, Pam Zeutchel and Ed and Betty Zeiger of the South Hill Sunrisers Kiwanis Club; Gina Sharpe of Shepherd of the Hill Presbyterian Church; Ruth Anderson; Gene Humiston Cotton; Art Foxford; Don and Mary Glaser; Bill Goelzer; Maybelle Hoenhous; Michael Kupfer; Don Massie; Dorothy Norris; Wes Perkinson; John Potter; Les Squires; Betsy Stubbs; Joan Vosler; Walt Zeiger; and Pete Ziemke.

Many thanks to acquisitions editor Laurie Krill and copy editor Ashley Hill of History Press for guiding this book to publication. Finally, we would like to thank Ruth and Andy Anderson of the Puyallup Historical Society, Paul Hackett, Erin Zeiger, Patricia Drake, Bob Ballou and Terry Maves for reviewing drafts of the manuscript and providing helpful feedback.

Hans Zeiger and Jerry Bates
Editors
South Hill, Washington

# BIBLIOGRAPHY

*Books and Articles*

Bonney, W.P. *History of Pierce County, Washington.* Chicago: Pioneer Historical Publishing Company, 1927.
Coen, Ross. *Fu-Go: The Curious History of Japan's Balloon Bomb Attack on America.* Lincoln: University of Nebraska Press, 2014.
DeRosa, Heather. "South Hill Historical Society Pieces Together Local History." *Puyallup Herald,* September 8, 2015. www.thenewstribune.com.
Drake, Patricia. "Persistence Pays Off as 40-Acre South Hill Park Set for Groundbreaking." *News Tribune,* March 26, 2000. B1.
———. "Six Spark Cityhood Campaign." *Pierce County Herald,* June 2, 1998. A1.
Hays, Otis, Jr. *Alaska's Hidden Wars: Secret Campaigns on the North Pacific Rim.* Fairbanks: University of Alaska Press, 2004.
Kawada, Eijiro. "Was South Hill Under Attack that Day in '45?" *News Tribune,* October 28, 2003. 1.
Mikesh, Robert C. *Japan's World War II Balloon Bomb Attacks on North America.* Washington, D.C.: Smithsonian Institution Press, 1973.
Needles, Allison. "Group Rallies to Protect Original Firgrove Elementary Building." *News Tribune,* April 13, 2018. www.thenewstribune.com.
———. "Meridian Habitat Park Playground Offers Nature Respite, Accessible Equipment for Kids." *Puyallup Herald,* Nov. 8, 2016, www.thenewstribune.com.
Price, Lori. "South Hill Schools Began in Log Cabin." *Pierce County Herald,* n.d.

# Bibliography

Price, Lori, and Ruth Anderson. *Puyallup: A Pioneer Paradise*. Charleston, SC: Arcadia Publishing, 2002.

*Tacoma Ledger*. Article on Firgrove School construction. September 25, 1935.

Vest, Carl. Various articles published in the *Puyallup Herald*, available at www.southhillhistory.com.

Weber, Bert. *Retaliation: Japanese Attacks and Allied Countermeasures on the Pacific Coast in World War II*. Corvallis: Oregon State University Press, 1975.

Zeiger, Hans. *Puyallup in World War II*. Charleston, SC: The History Press, 2018.

## *Documents*

Combs, Ernest, Bruce Mann and Michael Veseth. "An Economic Study of the Puyallup Valley–South Hill Area of Pierce County, Washington." University of Puget Sound Department of Economics, July 1977.

Commissioner of the General Land Office. Contract 138 (William Rankin Ballard). July 15, 1872.

Drake, Patricia. "Firgrove School History Information." 2018.

Gabrielson, Gabriel. Journal, 1930s–1940s. N.p.

Herbert, Cecil. "Woodland Bus Company, 1934–1952." Document in South Hill Historical Society collection.

Kupfer, Fred. Letters, 1942–1945. South Hill Historical Society Collection.

Mosolf, Edith Peters. "School District No. 114." 1936.

Pierce County. "Pierce County Comprehensive Plan, Appendix J: South Hill Community Plan." December 11, 2002, adopted June 2003. www.piercecountywa.org.

Pierce County Citizens. "Notice of Intention and Feasibility Study." Submitted to Pierce County Boundary Review Board, June 1998.

———. Petition to Pierce County Commissioners (for the creation of Ball-Wood Road), with survey and approval documents. Pierce County Archive, 1888.

———. Petition to Pierce County Commissioners to create Collins Road, with survey and approval documents. Pierce County Archive, 1892.

———. Petition to Pierce County Commissioners to create Glaser Road. Pierce County Archive, 1936.

———. Petition to Pierce County Commissioners to create Hemlock Road. Pierce County Archive, 1936.

———. Petition to Pierce County Commissioners to create Lundblad Road, with survey and approval documents. Pierce County Archive, 1928.

———. Petition to Pierce County Commissioners to create Muehler-Burger Road, with survey and approval documents. Pierce County Archive, 1889.

———. Petition to Pierce County Commissioners to create Odens Road, with survey and approval documents. Pierce County Archive, 1927.

Pierce County Council. Resolution No. R2011-14, "A Resolution of the Pierce County Council Celebrating the Tenth Anniversary of the South Hill Historical Society." 2011.

Pierce County Council. Resolution No. R2001-143, "A Resolution of the Pierce County Council and Executive Recognizing the Historic Significance of the South Hill Heritage Corridor; and Proclaiming the Day of October 11, 2011, to be 'South Hill Heritage Appreciation Day' in Pierce County, Washington." 2011.

South Hill Community Development Organization. Community Survey. March 1972.

South Hill Historical Society. Newsletters, April 2003–Summer 2019.

## *Maps*

Bates, Jerry. South Hill map graphics. South Hill Historical Society Collection.

Kroll. "T19NR4E." In *Kroll's Atlas of Pierce County, Washington*. 1915, 1917 and 1924 versions available in Tacoma Public Library, Northwest Room Collection.

Metzger, Charles F. *Township 19N, Range 4E. W.M.* 1924, 1936, 1941, 1951 and 1965 versions available in Tacoma Public Library, Northwest Room Collection.

Pierce County engineer. *TP 19N, R4E, W.M.* 1935.

Tacoma and Puyallup Railroad Co. *Fruitland*. 1891.

TICOR. *Rabbit Farms*. N.d.

U.S. Department of the Interior, Geological Survey. *Frederickson, Washington*. 1929.

U.S. Survey General's Office. *Township No. 19, North, Range 4 East, Willamette Meridian*. 1872 and 1874 versions available in the Washington State Historical Society Collection.

# Bibliography

## *Interviews*

*(Most records below are kept as video recordings by the South Hill Historical Society. Contact the South Hill Historical Society for more information.)*

Andrews, Daniel. South Hill Historical Society collection. July 13, 2013.

Bohrer, Babe Thun. Interview by Carl Vest and Paul Hackett. September 28, 2006.

Burnett, Marilyn Grace Herbert. South Hill Historical Society collection. March 13, 2005, n.d.

Cox, Ferne, and miscellaneous speakers. Interview by Paul Hackett. July 12, 2003.

Crabb, Robert Charles. Interview by Paul Hackett. July 10, 2002.

Cross, Stanley. Interview by Hans Zeiger. September 26, 2019.

Dahl, Niels M. Interviews by Paul Hackett. February 26, 2004, and March 5, 2004.

Daugherty, Robert G. Interview by Jeffrey Arnold. May 23, 2005.

De Salvo, Don. Interview by Hans Zeiger. October 16, 2019.

Dodd, Lloyd Lester. Interview by Paul Hackett. March 6 (year unknown).

Ellis, Joan. South Hill Historical Society collection. February 28, 2012, and May 19, 2012.

Elsdon, Thomas H., and Elaine E. Interview by Paul Hackett. November 12, 2001.

Frelin, Marjorie L. Greeley. Interview by Paul Hackett and Carolyn Nelson. October 22, 2001.

Gendreau, Fred. South Hill Historical Society collection. N.d.

Glaser, Don. Interview by Paul Hackett. September 10, 2001.

Goelzer, William David Lester. Interview by Paul Hackett. March 14, 2003.

Gogan, Pat. Interview by Paul Hackett. March 10, 2003.

Goheen, Hazel Whitford Miller. Interview by Paul Hackett. July 19, 2002.

———. South Hill Historical Society collection. January 7, 2005.

Goter, Stanley Eugene, and Ila Jean. South Hill Historical Society collection. October 19, 2004, and November 8, 2004.

Gould, Dorothy Enersole. Interview by Paul Hackett and Dan Andrews. March 8, 2004.

Gratzer, David Earl. South Hill Historical Society collection. November 3, 2003.

Herbert, Cecil V. South Hill Historical Society collection. March 13, 2005.

# Bibliography

Herbert, Cecil V., and Doris Johnson. South Hill Historical Society collection. N.d.
Hoenhous, Charles, and May Hoenhous. Interview by Paul Hackett. June 10, 2002.
Kee, Peter. South Hill Historical Society collection. N.d.
Kupfer, Paul. Interview by Paul Hackett. April 20, 2001.
Larson, Art. Interview by Hans Zeiger. June 11, 2019.
Massie, Arthur S., and Marvella A. Interview by Paul Hackett. April 21, 2002.
Massie, Marvella, and Dennis Massie. Interview by Paul Hackett and Terry Maves. February 26, 2013.
McDaniels, Leroy Alford. Interview by Paul Hackett. November 16, 2001.
Miller, Grace Irene Ritchie. South Hill Historical Society collection. February 14, 2001.
Moreland, Bob. Interview by Paul Hackett. January 15, 2008.
Mosolf, John. Interviews by Paul Hackett. April 9, 2001, May 17, 2001, and September 15, 2001.
———. South Hill Historical Society collection. January 20, 2004.
Nelson, Dorothy. South Hill Historical Society collection. April 26, 2013.
Nordin, Juanita Hale. Interview by Paul Hackett and Ben Peters. October 11, 2001.
Norris, Dorothy Swalander. Interview by Paul Hackett and Terry Maves. March 19, 2013.
O'Kelly, Chris, and Gloria George. Interview by Carl Vest. N.d.
Otto, Don. Interview by Ben Peters and Paul Hackett. April 16, 2004.
Otto, Don, and Helen Otto. Interview by Carl Vest and Paul Hackett. March 27, 2006.
———. Interview by Paul Hackett. Febrary 3, 2002.
Otto, Mike. South Hill Historical Society collection. August 21, 2001.
Parks family (children of Harold Parks). South Hill Historical Society collection. December 19, 2001, and February 4, 2002.
Parks, Peter. Interview by Carl Vest, Ben Peters and Jerry Bates. November 13, 2002.
Pendergrass, Lee. Interview by Paul Hackett. April 14, 2003.
Picha, Margaret Miller. Interviews by Paul Hackett. April 9, 2001, and April 14, 2001.
Robinson, Diny Thun. Interview by Carl Vest and Paul Hackett. November 13, 2002.
Rubger, Ann. South Hill Historical Society collection. October 28, 2013.
Ryan, Viva Louise Delano. Interview by Paul Hackett. October 10, 2002.

# Bibliography

Sagmiller, Dee. Interview by Carl Vest and Paul Hackett. May 31, 2006.
Shea, Gerald E. Interview by Paul Hackett. June 6, 2003.
Starkel, Bonnie Nicolet. Interview by Paul Hackett and Carl Vest. November 22, 2002.
Stoner, William Sanford. Interview by Paul Hackett. March 17, 2004.
Taylor, Robert P. Interview by Paul Hackett and Carl Vest. February 15, 2005.
Taylor, Robert P., and Jeanie Taylor. Interviews by Paul Hackett. July 6, 2004, and July 26, 2004.
Thun, John. Interview by Carl Vest and Paul Hackett. February 8, 2006.
Thun, John, and Bruce Thun. Interview by Paul Hackett. May 4, 2002.
Wassman, Carl. Interview by Paul Hackett. September 16, 2001.
Yeaw, Orlean A. Interview by Paul Hackett. April 8, 2003.
Ziemke, Pete. South Hill Historical Society collection. N.d.

## *Recorded Events*

Don and Helen Otto. Shed artifacts. July 3, 2006.
Firgrove School Reunion, Puyallup. September 12, 1986.
Good Samaritan Hospital's fiftieth Anniversary. December 6, 2002.
Heritage Day Walk. April 4, 2004.
John Mosolf's ninety-fifth Birthday Party. January 20, 2004.
Karshner Museum. "Camp Harmony: Understanding the Past." April 27, 2006.
———. Puyallup Preservation Day. May 1, 2004.
"My Hometown," featuring Bernice Rinehart and Olive Parks McDonough. May 2004.
"Nathan Chapman Memorial Trail Dedication (news segment)." Aired by KOMO 4 on July 18, 2005.
Olive Parks McDonald Memorial. September 9, 2014.
Pierce County. Sign Dedication Ceremony. October 11, 2001.
"Searching for the Wreck," the hunt for 1912 Interurban wreckage at Maplewood Springs. June 12, 2004.
South Hill Historical Society. "Ever Hear a Pig Squeal When Attacked by a Bear?" April 15, 2003.
———. "Firgrove School." March 20, 2012.
———. "Hilltop Auto Shop." October 29, 2015.
———. "Rabbit Farms." January 5, 2012.
———. Story Time. January 22, 2002, June 14, 2014, and March 17, 2015.

# Bibliography

———. "Viking and Shaw Road." November 15, 2016.
Thun Field Air Shows. Excerpt from a Win Brown video. 1963.
Wilhelm, Dorothy. *Welcome to My Hometown*. Aired by AT&T Broadband Community Television on December 1, 2001 and April 2005.
Woodland School Reunion. May 6, 2006.
Woodland School Reunion. May 5, 2012.

## *Recorded Presentations*

Anderson, Lawrence D. "Andy." May 21, 2013.
Anderson, Ruth, and John "Andy" Anderson. November 19, 2013.
Bails, Sherri. October 18, 2016.
Ballou, Helen C. August 18, 2003.
Ballou, Robert L. August 18, 2003.
Barandon, Nicole. April 19, 2016.
Barth, Dr. Charles. N.d.
Beal, Susan Gotchy. September 18, 2007.
Berger, Don. November 15, 2011.
Bobb, Richard. February 20, 2007.
Bod, Curt. November 18, 2008.
Boettcher, Werner. September 16, 2008.
Burnett, Marilyn Grace Herbert. January 13, 2003.
Burtnett, Debbie. October 20, 2009.
Christy, Dorothy Pearson. May 16, 2004.
Cox, Vernon Royal. June 16, 2009.
Cross, Stanley. March 11, 2004, and January 19, 2011.
Crowe, Dick. May 17, 2011.
Dalke, Helen Lavonne Scott. October 17, 2004.
Dally, Ray. May 18, 2010.
Dixon, Jim. March 11, 2001.
Dixon, Loretta. March 11, 2001.
Dixon, Richard M. March 11, 2001.
Drake, Patricia. March 18, 2008.
Fox, Steve. January 21, 2014.
Foxford, Art. February 17, 2009, and April 21, 2015.
Foxford, Luverne. February 17, 2009.
Goelzer, Roger Allen. April 22, 2002.
Goelzer, Wilma Meeds. April 22, 2002.

# BIBLIOGRAPHY

Greeley, Warner. August 6, 2010.
Hackett, Dave. June 16, 2015.
Hansen, Reed. March 19, 2001.
Harvey, JoAnn. April 15, 2008.
Harvey, Neal R. April 15, 2008.
Herbert, Cecil. January 13, 2003, and March 15, 2005.
Hess, Karen. October 21, 2014.
Hoenhous, Joe. March 21, 2017.
Hoenhous, Maybelle. March 21, 2017.
Hopp, Ernie. March 8, 2005.
Hopp, Irene. March 8, 2005.
Houk, Ruth Shannon. November 15, 2005.
Hultquist, Carl Gustaf, and Leona Hultquist. January 23, 2004.
Kehr, Bruce. January 13, 2007.
Kessler, Donald. May 17, 2005.
Klingenstein, Shane. March 20, 2007.
Larsen, Albert Andy. December 7, 2001.
Larsen, Chuck. April 15, 2014.
Larsen, Dennis. April 16, 2017.
Larson, Art. January 22, 2004, January 17, 2006, May 20, 2008, and September 17, 2013.
Larson, Lorraine. January 22, 2004.
Mann, Jeff. May 16, 2017.
Maves, Terry. October 15, 2013.
May, Deanna Gotchy. September 18, 2007.
McCarty, Deryl. February 21, 2017.
Moe, Ronald. February 21, 2008.
Nelson, Dorothy. February 19, 2013.
Nimick, Chris. May 15, 2012.
Norris, Dorothy Swalander. May 14, 2002, and January 17, 2006.
O'Kelly, Mike. March 18, 2008.
Otto, Don. January 17, 2006.
Paris, John. March 16, 2004.
Parks, Peter. May 19, 2009.
Pearson, Ronald D. May 21, 2003, and February 21, 2006.
Pearson, William E. May 16, 2004.
Ramsey, Jerry. May 18, 2016.
Reynon, Brandon. April 19, 2016.
Rinehart, Bernice M. May 19, 2003, and May 21, 2003.

Rockstad, Vern. April 16, 2008, September 20, 2011, and September 15, 2015.
Rodahl, Dave. March 16, 2004.
Root, Earl Stanley. February 25, 2004.
Rushton, Maudine Swalander. May 14, 2002.
Scott, William Harold. October 17, 2004.
Soros, Susan Inman. May 14, 2002.
Starkel, Elsie. January 9, 2004.
Stover, William. November 19, 2007.
Stubbs, Betsy. September 20, 2016.
Thorpe, Ralph. January 17, 2006.
Thun, John. June 8, 2005.
Trever, Jade. February 17, 2015.
Vest, Carl. January 25, 2014.
Vosler, Joan Parks. December 17, 2013.
Wimsett, Kevin. February 15, 2005.
Wirsing, Dale. May 19, 2015.
Zeiger, Edward. February 19, 2013.
Zeiger, Karl. November 20, 2012.
Zulauf, Allen. April 16, 2013, and March 18, 2014.

## *Websites*

Cafaro Company. "South Hill Mall." www.cafarocompany.com.
Facebook. "Puyallup Dragway." www.facebook.com.
National Park Service. "4-Trails Feasibility Study: The Oregon Trail Study Routes." www.nps.gov.
Pierce County. "South Hill Community Plan Update." www.co.pierce.wa.us.
Puyallup School District. "Bond and Levy History." www.puyallupsd.ss11.sharpschool.com.
Tarragon Property Services. "Sunrise Village." www.tarragon.com.

# INDEX

**A**

Adrain, Mrs. 117
Alderton 24
Allen, E.C. 38
Allen, Paul 168
Ancient Klickitat Trail 11, 12
Annis, Howard 106
Arabella Business Park 148
Atinnette, F.M. 71
Aylen, Dr. Charles 105

**B**

Bailets, C.D. 71
Bails, Sherri 167, 175
Balck, Fritz 19
Ballard, William Rankin 16, 18
Ball, Harvey M. 71
Ballou, Bob 69
Ballou, Frank 60, 104, 113, 114
Ballou Junior High School 104, 116, 158
Ball-Wood Road (see also Meridian) 8, 26, 31, 59, 73, 77, 81
Barth, Fred, Jr. 35
Barth, Fred, Sr. 35
Barth, Henry 35
Barth, Louis 165
Barth, Margaretha 35
Barth, William 35
Bennett, Katie Gabrielson 69
Bethany Baptist Church 177
Biles, James 13
Bill, Willard 107
Bock, Mrs. 62
Bone, Senator Homer 110
Bradley Lake 11, 25, 165, 166
Bradley, Ward 165
Breckon, Rufle 65
Brown, George 18

**C**

Callahan, Dora 117
Cedar Swamp 47, 48, 49, 82
Central Pierce Fire and Rescue 151, 152
Chapman, SFC Nathan 170
Clifford, Guy 76
Coyne, Sally 97
Crabb, Bob 38, 107
Crabtree, Martin 107
Crabtree, Ronald 38

# INDEX

## D

Daugherty, Lynne  54
Daugherty, Robert  54
Davidson, Edna  117
Deagan, Margaret  59
Delano, Al  49, 52, 94, 136
Dobbs, Mildred Heil  38
Dolph, Jeannette  97
Donation Land Claim Act of 1850  12, 18, 70
Drake, Pat  167, 168
Dumblar, Anton  17

## E

Edgerton, Miles  67
Edgerton, M.S.  31
Emerald Ridge High School  7, 87, 177
Emma Carson Elementary School  177
Environmental Protection Agency  161

## F

Federal Aviation Administration  157
Ferrucci, Vitt  157
Finley, Reverend Joe, Jr.  115
Finnestad, Larry  167
Firgrove Community Baptist Church  116
Firgrove Mutual Water Company  149, 150
Firgrove School  9, 58, 59, 65, 69, 83, 88, 101, 104, 111, 113, 125, 147, 194
Floyd, Don  46
Floyd, Frank  46
Floyd, Temple  46
Forest Grove School  65, 66, 68, 112
Foxford, Art  37
Foxford, LuAnne  167
Fruitland Avenue  38, 41, 64
Fruitland Grange  64, 65, 99, 101, 109, 111, 113, 116
Fullager, Charles  67

## G

Gabrielson, Emily  32, 34
Gabrielson, Gabe  35
Gabrielson, Gabriel  34
Gabrielson, Margie  32
Gabrielson, Ole  32, 34
Garden of Eden Nursery  127, 128
Gaspard, Marc  167
Geddes, Bill  65
Geddes, Myra  65
Geiger, Joseph  19
Gem Heights  130
Gendreau, Fred  124
Gendreau, Sandra Inman  124
George Edgerton Elementary School  177
Gilliland's Grocery  38
Glacier View Junior High School  177
Glaser, Don  39, 60, 69, 87, 88, 102
Glaser, Joe  39
Glaser, Mary  61, 69, 88
Glaser, Nicholas  79
Goelzer, Bill  39, 51
Goelzer, Faye  38
Goelzer, Lester  38
Goelzer, Patty Van Horn  38
Goelzer, William, Sr.  68
Goheen, Hazel Whitford Miller  38, 62, 65
Goings, Calvin  168, 170
Goodner, Erma  117
Good Samaritan Hospital  124, 148
Gould, Wilber F.  82
Graham  11, 65, 72, 73, 102, 113, 151
Graham, Reverend Billy  128
Grimm, Dan  167
Growth Management Act  172
"Gut" Johnson's Tallow Works  38

## H

Hackett, Paul  116, 131, 160
Hale, C.C.  67
Hall, James  19
Harrison, Kee  31

## Index

Hartman, Frank  31
Headly, Thomas  18
Heil, Helena  38, 117
Heinz, Mr.  107
Herbert, W.H.  85
Hidden Valley Landfill  161, 162
Hilderbrand, Bill  89
Hilderbrand, Eliza Ellen  89
Hilderbrand, Jim  89
Hilderbrand, Minetta  89
Hilderbrand, Phoebe  89
Hilderbrand, William  89, 90
Hoenhous, Alan  138
Hoenhous, Chuck  135, 138
Hoenhous, Joe  138
Hoenhous, Maybelle  135
Homestead Act of 1862  18
Hooper, Janelle  167
House of Kee  126
Hudson Bay Company  12
Huff, Barbara  38
Huff, Winnifred  62

## J

Jackson, Mr.  64
Jackson, Mrs.  64
Jehovah's Witnesses (South Hill congregation)  116
"Jesus of Nazareth" (play)  174
John R. Rogers High School  7, 13, 48, 49, 68, 69, 102, 157, 158, 160, 167

## K

Kee, Peter  126
Kehr, Faye C.  105
Kincaid, J.C.  71
Knapp, Mr.  64
Knapp, Mrs.  64
Knoll, Ruth Lillian Sharpe  42
Korum, Jerry  177
Korum, Mel  177
Kupfer, Alois  20, 22, 67
Kupfer, F.L.  31
Kupfer, Fred, Jr.  94
Kupfer, Lizzie  67, 68
Kupfer, Louis  31, 67
Kupfer, Mary  94, 97
Kupfer, Paul  97
Kupfer, Ruth  97

## L

Lane, Daniel  18
Larson, Art  157, 158
LeMay, Harold E.  160
Leonard, James  19
Lester, Rose  54
Letourneau, Dick  107
Lighthouse Christian Center  177
Lincoln, President Abraham  24
Litton, Robert  64
Living Hope Church  115
Longmire, James  13
Lyman, Mr.  83

## M

Manorwood  41, 128, 130
Mardock, Reverend Ike  115
Martin, Joel  31
Massie, Arthur  98
Massie, Charles Anion  98
McMillin  19, 91
McMillin Reservoir  34
Meeker, Ezra  41, 55, 79
Mel Korum Family YMCA  7
Mercy, George  71, 72
Meridian Habitat Park  174, 189
Meridian Riding Club  107
Miller, A.N.  67
Miller, Charles  16
Miller, Clifford  65
Miller, Faye  65
Miller, Nancy  106
Mitchell-Gould Road (152nd Street)  81, 82, 83
Moreland Tree Farms  125
Mosolf, Antoinie  22
Mosolf, Ennie  22

# INDEX

Mosolf, George  22, 67
Mosolf, George, Jr.  22
Mosolf, John  22, 66, 67
Mosolf, Joseph  22
Mosolf, Mrs.  35
Mosolf, Theresa  22
Muehler, Agnes  26
Muehler, Albin  26
Muehler-Berger Road  8
Muehler, Carl  18, 26, 70
Muehler, Carl F.  25
Muehler, Louisa  26
Muehler, Otto  26
Muehler, S.  26
Murray, Senator Patty  175

## N

Naches Pass Trail  13, 15, 16, 19, 31, 32, 206
Nelson, Dorothy  63
Newcomb, Robert  6
Newcomer, George  7
Nicholson, S.C.  67
Nicolet, John "Jack"  102, 104
Nolan, Helen  41
Nolan, Stephen  41
Norm's Auto Wrecking  137
Norris, Dorothy Swalander  28, 49
Northern Pacific Railroad  23, 24, 32, 59

## O

Obama, President Barack  15
O'Kelly, Chris  84
O'Kelly, Gloria George  83
Old Line Trolley (Tacoma Railway and Power Co. Line)  74
Our Savior Lutheran Church  116

## P

Park, Perle  63
Parks, Harold R.  53
Parks, Orin  98

Patzner, Florence  58
Patzner, John Joseph  58
Patzner, Mrs.  62
Pope Elementary School  46, 61, 90, 98, 180
Powers, Orvis  31
Predmore, Mr.  62
Predmore, Mrs.  64
Price, William  67
Puyallup Chamber of Commerce  73, 134
Puyallup Fruit and Garden Tracts  42
Puyallup Heights Community Club  111, 112
Puyallup Heights Improvement Club  68, 73, 112
Puyallup Heights School  65
Puyallup High School  69
Puyallup Tribe  11

## R

Rabbit Farms  6, 41, 44, 45, 46, 63, 69
Raymoure, Veriin  71
Reich, Jessica  54
Repp, Captain James, Jr.  56
Reynolds' Grocery  137
Rinehart, Betty  65
Rinehart, Roy  65
Rogers, Governor John R.  157
Rohlman, Helen Heil  38
Rupp, Pastor  115

## S

Sagmiller, James  154
Sane, Edward  19
Serviss, Faye Miller  65
Serviss, Frank  65
Sharpe family  43
Shaw, Chris  75, 76, 77
Shaw, Emery  75
Shaw, Frank  75, 76, 78
Shaw, Mrs. C.B.  77
Shaw Road  45, 74, 76, 77, 78, 87, 127

# INDEX

Shea, Eva  41
Shea, Michael  41, 43
Shepherd of the Hill Presbyterian Church  116, 131
Shuman, William  71
Smith, Carol Parks  38, 98
Smith, Pat Hoenhous  138
Smith, R.E.  85
South Hill Action to Protect the Environment  174
South Hill Athletic Association  134
South Hill Baptist Church  116
South Hill Community Council  142, 174, 175, 207
South Hill Community Development Organization  134
South Hill Heritage Corridor  14
South Hill Land Use Advisory Committee  173
South Hill Library  162, 205
South Hill Mall  44, 49, 107, 137, 139
South Hill Outdoor Recreation and Education (SHORE)  167
South Hill-Summit View Community Council  170
Southview (cityhood campaign)  170, 171
Spencer, John  71
Starkel, Bonnie Nicolet  49
Starkel, Dave  49
Starkel Turkey Farm  136
Starvation Valley Garbage  161
State Route 512  11, 36, 107, 130, 142, 177
Steele, Myra  89
Steele, Myra Hilderbrand  89, 90
Steele, Robert  89
Stover, Eunice  63
Strandley, Betty  38
Strandley, Eleanor  38
Strandley, Lillian  38
Stubbs, Betsy  174
Sunrise Elementary School  61, 180
Sunrise (housing development)  47, 177
Sunrisers' South Hill Kiwanis Club  138
Sunrise Village  31, 123
Sutherland, Doug  168
Swalander, Carl  28, 29
Swalander, Maude  117
Swalander, Oscar  53
Swalander, Rheinhold  28, 29

## T

Tacoma & Puyallup Railroad Company  42
Tallant, J.E.  33
Taylor, Herbert  68
Templin, Ann  117
Templin brothers  38
Tesso, Jim  170
Thomas, L.H.  61
Thorpe, Ralph  54
Thorpe, Yvonne  54
Thun Field  25, 69, 111, 152, 161, 173
Thun, John  152, 156
Township 19A Association (T19A)  131
Turnmire, J.H.  83
Tuttle, Virginia  117

## V

VanderPas, Lori  170
VanderPas, William J.  170
Van Horn, Mildred  38
Van Pevenage, Albert  36
Vosler, Joan Parks  38, 69, 98

## W

Walcott, Jan  168
Walk, George  167
Walmart (store)  154, 177
Washington State Department of Transportation  157
Waterbury, Chantel  127
Weyerhaeuser Timber Company  24, 31, 32, 83
Wildwood Park Elementary School  61
Williams, Julia  38

# INDEX

Williams, Lynn  38
Williams, Nellie  117
Willows Corner  6, 20, 25, 44, 49, 51,
    88, 94, 102, 106, 125
Willows Dance Hall  6, 51, 52, 73
Willows Lumber  6, 135, 136, 137, 138
Willows Shopping Center  49, 53
Willows Tavern  6, 92
Wilson, Christine  170
Women's Benefit Association  114
Woodland Avenue  14, 38, 41, 42, 48,
    74, 161
Woodland Bus Company  84, 85, 86, 190
Woodland Gospel Temple  115
Woodland School  37, 41, 42, 43, 55,
    56, 57, 63, 102, 110, 111, 117
Woolery, Daniel  19

## Z

Zeiger, Edward  61
Ziemke, Linda  78
Ziemke, Pete  78, 127, 129
Zimmerman, Fred  30
Zimmerman, Louis  30
Zimmerman, Mary  30
Zulauf, Allen  141
Zulauf, Ellen  142

# ABOUT THE SOUTH HILL HISTORICAL SOCIETY

The idea for the South Hill Historical Society arose from several meetings of the Friends of the South Hill Library. The librarian expressed frustration at the dearth of material on local history. High school teachers were assigning students research projects, and the library had no way to help them. Several people expressed interest in doing something to help the librarian. They debated a number of ideas. Eventually, in 2001, Paul Hackett, Ben Peters and Carl Vest decided to create a historical society. The three founders agreed to undertake various roles to make it happen. A grant of one hundred dollars from the Friends of the Library provided the funds from which the historical society was created.

The society started a research program that involved identifying longtime residents and videotaping interviews with them. That effort has been very successful, and the society has nearly two hundred taped conferences with longtime Hill people, some of whom are now deceased. An effort was initiated to gather family histories and other written materials from older residents; this, too, has been successful, and many of these histories are now in the society's archives. The society assembled a collection of

## About the South Hill Historical Society

maps and representative artifacts, including old road signs and handmade embroidery work.

Over time, as new members joined the society, a newsletter, edited by Jerry Bates, was circulated; it has been published since 2003. Monthly meetings of the society's members have been scheduled for years, and a wide variety of speakers have appeared before the group. Carl Vest wrote a monthly newspaper column for the *Puyallup Herald* about South Hill History from 2007 to 2017.

The society also maintains an active online presence. Jerry Bates has created a website, www.southhillhistory.com, and posted all of the newsletters and various writings on it. The reach of these postings has been amazing. Requests for more information have come in from all over the world. In recent years, for example, Jerry has received inquiries about burials from a group in Germany that explores the histories of German immigrants who settled on South Hill.

The members of the society's officer group are regularly asked to speak before local civic crowds and other organizations. The society also works closely with national groups, such as the Oregon-California-Trails Association, to help establish the Naches Pass Trail as part of the National Trails System.

On the occasion of its tenth anniversary, the Pierce County Council issued a proclamation commending the organization for its work.

## Jerry Bates

Jerry Bates has been editor of the South Hill Historical Society newsletter since 2003 and is the society's website designer. He graduated from Puyallup High School in 1965 and served in the U.S. Army for three years. After leaving the military, he earned associate degrees from Green River College and Tacoma Community College with studies at the Los Angeles Art Center. He spent his career as a graphic designer for the Boeing Company, working within the industrial engineering department for the 757-737 programs. After living most of his life on South Hill and seeing many changes, he joined the South Hill Historical Society shortly after retirement.

## Hans Zeiger

Hans Zeiger is a local historian, author and member of the Pierce County Council. A state legislator from 2011 to 2020, Hans was a trustee of the Washington State Historical Society and a member of the Washington State Legislative Oral History Advisory Board. His writings on history have appeared in the *Puyallup Herald*, *Columbia* magazine and *HistoryLink*, and he is the author of *Puyallup in World War II*, available from The History Press. The son, grandson and great-grandson of Puyallup educators, Hans lives with his family on South Hill.

# ABOUT THE AUTHOR AND EDITORS

### Carl R. Vest

Carl Vest, PhD, is the research director and cofounder of the South Hill Historical Society. He wrote a regular column on South Hill history for the *Puyallup Herald* for a decade. He previously served as the president of the South Hill Community Council.

As a U.S. Air Force veteran with service in the Philippines, the Berlin Airlift and the Korean War, Carl went on to a distinguished career in scientific and technical research. He was an engineer and design team member for missile detection and satellite weather systems at General Electric from 1955 to 1962. He was also a government technical liaison for GE in the 1960s. From 1972 to 1992, Carl was a social and biological sciences consultant at Battelle Memorial Institute. He finished his professional career as a professor of quantitative decision making at Marymount University School of Business in the 1990s.

Carl holds a BS from Virginia Polytechnic Institute, an MS from George Washington University and a PhD from American University. Now retired, Carl and his wife, Lea, reside on South Hill. Carl served as the president of the South Hill-Summit View Community Council and as the president of the Gem Heights Homeowners Association. He is a member of the Kiwanis Club of Puyallup.